SPECIAL NEEDS IN MAINSTREAM SCHOOLS

Series Editor: Keith Postlethwaite

CLASSROOM RESPONSES TO LEARNING DIFFICULTIES

Bridie Raban and Keith Postlethwaite

MACMILLAN
EDUCATION

First published 1988

Published by
MACMILLAN EDUCATION LTD
Houndmills, Basingstoke, Hampshire RG21 2XS
and London
Companies and representatives
throughout the world

Printed in Hong Kong

ISBN 0–333–43918–X

Contents

1

2

3

4

8

9

vi

This book was produced by the Special Needs Research Team within the Oxford Educational Research Group. Team members were Beverley Davies, James Gray, Ann Hackney, Keith Postlethwaite and Bridie Raban. This book was prepared for the research team by Bridie Raban and Keith Postlethwaite. The book, which is one of a series of three, is one product of a research project that was funded by the Rayne Foundation and based at the University of Oxford, Department of Educational Studies.

Preface

This book and its companion volumes are intended for teachers and student teachers interested in mainstream secondary education. This volume deals with responses which an individual teacher can make in his or her own classroom to support pupils who have learning difficulties. The other volumes deal with classroom responses to behavioural difficulties and with the organisational response of the whole school to that fifth of its pupils who have special educational needs.

The approach taken in the series is based on the idea that special needs can only be adequately met in schools if all teachers recognise that they have a role to play and if all are able to develop some appropriate skills. This starting point does not negate the importance of specialist provision from special needs departments – indeed much of the volume on organisational responses deals specifically with how such departments might operate. However, we do firmly believe that without an element of response from every teacher, there are severe limitations on what a special needs department can achieve.

In this book we concentrate on the issue of supporting pupils with learning difficulties. The aim is to help mainstream teachers extend the range of strategies which they can use in their own classrooms and to improve the interchange of information between mainstream and special needs staff.

The general approach of the book is a practical one, with suggestions for activities which a teacher might do. So that these stand out in the text, we have used a tinted background for activity suggestions with an **A** in the margin. Information and summaries of key points are highlighted between heavy horizontal lines, with an **i** in the margin.

We hope the book will be useful to individual teachers or students working on their own, to groups following formal pre-service and in-service training courses and to ad hoc groups that might come together in individual schools to explore, as a group of colleagues, some of the most fascinating and demanding tasks which we have to undertake as teachers.

K.C.P.
OXFORD 1987

Acknowledgements

Many of the activities suggested in this book are not new. We are happy to acknowledge our indebtedness to many colleagues for the ideas which we have presented. We would especially like to thank Helen Arnold (Homerton College, Cambridge), Diana Bentley (University of Reading), Charles Cripps (Institute of Education, Cambridge), Florence Davies (University of Birmingham), Elizabeth Goodacre (Middlesex Polytechnic), Marilyn Leah (King Alfred's College, Winchester), Albert Morris (Brisbane College of Advanced Education), Greg Robinson (Newcastle College of Advanced Education), Olive Robinson (Oxford Polytechnic) and Nea Stewart-Dore (Brisbane College of Advanced Education).

We were also greatly assisted in preparing this book by representatives from the University Departments of Education in England and Wales who met together on several occasions in London and in Oxford, to discuss our research programme in general and these materials in particular.

Our colleagues in the Oxford Department of Educational Studies have contributed a great deal to the book, through the general discussions which we were able to have with them and through the constructive, supportive, yet properly critical atmosphere which exists here. In particular we would like to thank Elizabeth Hitchfield for much helpful comment and general support.

Another major influence has been the group of teachers, with interests and expertise in the special needs field, who were seconded to Oxford during the period of our research programme. Our discussions with them have helped enormously to clarify our ideas and extend the range of the teaching strategies which we have been able to describe.

The chapter on difficulties in mathematics owes much to two groups of teachers, advisers and University colleagues who met in Oxford and in Reading to help us with this issue. To these groups, we are enormously grateful.

We also owe a considerable debt to the three year-groups of PGCE students in Oxford who suffered earlier versions of these materials and whose reactions have helped us to develop them to the present state.

Finally, we must thank out editor at Macmillan, Elizabeth Paren, whose ideas and suggestions have been of great help and whose reminders about deadlines have been far gentler than we deserve.

Introduction

The major impact of the Warnock Report (DES, 1978) has been to point out the range and variety of need which is evident among pupils requiring some special educational provision. The report also argued that such provision is not solely the responsibility of teachers in separate schools, nor is it solely the responsibility of special needs specialists in mainstream schools. Indeed, Warnock suggested that *all* teachers in mainstream schools need to have relevant skills and information to identify and provide for pupils with special educational needs.

Extreme cases of special need are easy to identify although it is not always obvious how to meet these needs appropriately. This group can include pupils with severe learning difficulties (e.g. those often associated with Down's Syndrome or cerebral palsy), highly disruptive pupils and pupils with physical or sensory disorders (e.g. the child with spina bifida, or the deaf or partially hearing child). Though categories of handicap and labels such as these can be useful in general discussions they have the disadvantage of stereotyping the provision and can hide from us the real requirements of individual pupils. Labels imply similarities between pupils in a given category, whereas the educational needs of two partially hearing pupils, say, may be very different. Labels also emphasise differences between the categories of handicap which may not be appropriate, for similar forms of provision may be useful and similar organisational problems may arise in trying to help pupils in all these categories. More importantly, pupils frequently have more than one disability, and their major handicap as defined in medical terms, for example, may not be their most significant difficulty from an educational point of view. Lastly, there is the problem that category labels remain with pupils long after their value has ceased and this can be damaging to progress for some pupils.

Less extreme cases are not so easy to identify and therefore they are more vulnerable to inappropriate or inadequate provision, or indeed to having no special provision made for them at all. Such pupils can easily be dismissed as badly behaved or slow learning and remain underachievers throughout their school careers. This group includes pupils who have difficulty with reading or writing for example, or pupils whose basic language skills are adequate but who have difficulties with the concepts of a particular subject. It also includes pupils who have transferred from a different school with a different syllabus, who might need help catching up. These are just examples from the wide range of needs which pupils might have. Categories of handicap can, of course, be used again in these less extreme cases, but all the disadvantages of categories which we discussed in the previous paragraph can still apply.

The Warnock Report identified one in five pupils as having special educational needs at one time or another in our schools. It is clear, therefore, that special needs pupils form a large group in the school population. However, it is also clear that this group is not homogeneous. The different *kinds* of special need mentioned above is one source of variety in the group. Another, also discussed above, is the *severity* of the need. Within each type of need, some pupils' difficulties are severe or even profound, whereas other pupils have moderate or mild difficulties. Thus, of the group of pupils with reading difficulties, some will be unable to read at all whereas others will have difficulty in understanding and retaining information from their reading. Finally there is the notion of the *persistence* of pupils' needs. Some pupils will have needs which remain throughout their school life and beyond. Others' needs may be of short duration. These three dimensions of type, severity and persistence are quite independent of one another with the implication that special needs pupils differ greatly and that special needs provision must be very flexible.

Special needs provision of adequate scale and flexibility cannot be left to a small number of special needs teachers in a large secondary school. Such teachers have an important role as expert advisers to mainstream staff and as sources of direct support for some special needs pupils, especially those with the most severe or complex difficulties. However, some responsibility in terms of identification and provision for the whole range of pupils with special needs inevitably rests with mainstream teachers both as subject teachers and form tutors. This is particularly the case because only some aspects of special needs are related to low general ability. Pupils with special needs therefore appear in all classes.

This has implications for your own teaching and how you think about that. Remember that in categorising pupils we are in danger of implying that special educational needs arise because of some deficit on the part of the pupil. A more realistic way of thinking about special needs is to see them as arising out of the interaction between the characteristics of the pupil on the one hand and those of the education system as it is organised, on the other. As far as the characteristics of the system are concerned, the way you choose materials and teach lessons can be at least as significant as the way schools, LEAs or government make the large scale decisions.

This interactionist model should encourage us to engage in a twofold approach towards special needs:

1. To make appropriate *special* provision in our own classrooms and through special needs departments so that these pupils can benefit from their experience of school as it is organised at present.

2. To think hard about how the *normal* practice and organisation of schools and of classrooms can be modified to reduce special needs, e.g. by being more responsive towards individual differences between pupils in the school as a whole.

These are far-reaching suggestions. One is therefore tempted to ask whether the time and energy that would be required to put them into practice can be justified. Fish (1985) provides an important insight into this issue. He argues that the search for higher standards in schools as a whole can lead in two directions. One results in a narrower common curriculum, a less flexible approach towards individual needs and the stigmatisation of pupils who are 'not up to standard'. In this context special provision is held to be merely charitable provision for failures, and the twofold approach outlined above would indeed be difficult to justify. However, Fish's second route to improved standards lies in the better matching of tasks, objectives and materials to individuals. In this line of thought, the twofold approach to special needs work can be seen as the most refined application of the philosophy of the school as a whole, as a major element in the improvement of education for all pupils, and therefore as readily justifiable.

These general points are discussed in more detail in the book in this series which deals with the organisation of special needs systems in schools. The present book has been put together to help you to increase your own awareness of, and competence in working with, special needs pupils in your own lessons. Much of what is suggested here can be implemented in any school, whatever formal organisational response is being pursued. It is aimed at helping you to fulfil your own responsibilities as a teacher of those pupils with special needs who are to be found in your classes. In particular, this book concentrates on helping you to be more effective in meeting the needs of the groups of pupils whose problems are essentially *learning difficulties*.

The main part of the book provides specific advice on particular difficulties. However, it is also important to think more widely about pupils with learning difficulties. The broader activities in Activity 1.1 on page 4 will help you to do this.

The suggestions in Activity 1.1 will give you some general insights into the problems of pupils who have learning difficulties and to ways of helping them. In the rest of this book we will explore these problems in more detail.

We will tackle this in three stages:

1. Identification and diagnosis
You need to know *which* pupils have learning difficulties and *what*, precisely, these difficulties are.

● See chapter 2

2. Provision
You need to know what *you* can do in the context of your own classroom.

● See chapters 3–7

3. Support
You need to know where to get help from colleagues in school and how to get the most from your discussions with these colleagues.

● See chapter 8

Chapter 9 gives a summary of general points to remember and describes a model of teaching which might help you to think more about the special needs aspect of the teacher's job.

There is another book in this series which deals with classroom responses to disruptive behaviour in the same sort of way (*Classroom Responses to Disruptive Behaviour*).

Activity 1.1
Background activities

1. With the help of other teachers, identify one or two pupils with learning difficulties in one of your classes. Keep a diary of your involvement with them. For a period of 2–3 weeks do this in as much detail as you can, noting such things as how you intend to provide for them in your lessons and what the outcomes are.

After several weeks ask yourself what you could find out about the pupils' difficulties in the context of the class, what sorts of teaching strategies you were able to use and what proved to be successful.

2. Arrange to do several sessions of individual tuition with a pupil in your own subject. It may be a pupil who finds the subject hard, or it may be a pupil who has transferred from another set or a different school and needs help to catch up. You may need to take the advice of your colleagues over what kind of arrangement – if any – is practical in your school, but this work *could* take place in a short session during the lunch break, or you may be able to provide the extra help during lesson time (e.g. if a colleague is willing to let you take the pupil from his or her lesson at a time when you are free). Make a note of the pupil's needs (the checklists which follow may help you to decide what these are – as may discussion with colleagues). Note also your aims for tuition, your objectives for each session, how you set about achieving them and what outcomes emerge.

What were you able to find out about the pupil's difficulties in the one-to-one situation? What strategies were you able to use in this situation? What was successful? How could the experiences of one-to-one tuition be transferred to your class teaching?

3. If you teach a pupil who has help from the special needs department in your school, find out what kind of help is provided, and how it is organised. Also ask about ways in which you could complement this work in your own lessons. A good way of getting these kinds of information is to ask the pupil's other teachers, their form tutor and the special needs staff. (See also Chapter 8 of this book.) Remember that the child may not be keen to talk to you about getting extra help.

How does the special needs department function in your school? How could you relate your own work more closely to that of the department so that a coherent pattern of support is offered to the pupil? What sorts of information on individual pupils and on your own subject can you provide for the special needs department so that its work can be better focused and more effective?

Identification and diagnosis of special educational needs

2

The identification of pupils with special educational needs does not have to be a particularly lengthy or complicated procedure. Indeed, it is part of the everyday work of the classroom teacher.

2.1 Quick identification

You will find Activity 2.1 useful in alerting you to pupils with learning difficulties.

Activity 2.1
Word list
Choose ten words which refer to key concepts from the topic you are working on. Check that the pupils can a) read these words, b) write these words, and c) understand what these words mean. These checks can be easily arranged by duplicating a list of the words and asking the pupils to copy them into their books and, alongside, to fill in their own understanding of the meaning. Pupils can be invited to tick the words they feel confident in reading for themselves. They can put a cross against words they haven't seen before. Also check, from time to time, to see if they can copy such words accurately from the blackboard as this necessary skill is more difficult than copying from a sheet of paper on the desk.

Do this regularly and follow up any pupils who seem to be in difficulty. One form of follow up is through the use of the checklists which we introduce on page 7.

Your general observation of pupils in class, and your marking of pupils' written work, will also help to identify pupils who seem to be having difficulty. This will be a more reliable element in your quick identification process if you have given some thought to what you would expect pupils of a given age to be able to do in your subject. You are then less likely to be misled by low standards on what was actually a rather unrealistic piece of work, by particularly neat or scruffy pieces of work, or by pupils with especially good or bad attitudes to work. Developing lists of expectations of this kind can be a very worthwhile exercise to undertake with a group of colleagues. In some subject areas (for example, mathematics and science) the

6

reports of the Assessment of Performance Unit (e.g. APU 1980; 1981; 1982a; 1982b) can be helpful starting points.

Additional insights about pupils can come from test results or the opinions of other subject teachers. Poor results on subject tests, reports of difficulty in other subjects from other teachers, or poor results on any general screening tests that are used in your school (for example, IQ tests or reading age tests) should alert you to *possible* learning difficulties. Equally, unexpectedly high results in screening tests, or high performance in other subjects that might be reported by colleagues, might suggest that the pupil is underachieving in your subject and, therefore, that he or she has some problem in relation to that subject or to your approach to teaching it.

Like pupils identified by the word list activity, pupils who come to light through observation, through written work assessment, or through test-based screening, should be followed up by more detailed investigation. Again, one way of doing this by the use of checklists is discussed below. It may also be necessary, subsequently, to discuss the pupil with other staff such as those with special responsibility for pupils with special educational needs. Ideas for structuring such conversations are presented in Chapter 8.

2.2 Use of checklists

You may identify most of the pupils with learning difficulties through using the combination of procedures outlined above. However, you will not yet have a clear picture of the nature of their difficulties.

This can be obtained by using the checklists which follow. The checklists show in more detail exactly what the difficulty *is* for the pupil – that is, the checklists act as 'diagnostic' instruments.

The *first* checklist will help you to identify the kinds of language difficulties which a pupil may have in learning your particular *subject*. The *second* checklist, which can of course be applied to the same pupil, will give you further information which will indicate whether or not that pupil's language difficulties are of a more *general* nature.

There will be other things specifically related to your subject that may cause difficulty for a pupil, for example:

- numerical ability;
- other aspects of mathematical ability;
- the hierarchy of concepts in your subject;
- manipulative skills in practical lessons;
- drawing skills;
- co-ordination skills.

The key points will clearly vary from subject to subject so you will need to develop your own, Subject Specific Checklist.

Activity 2.2
Developing your own checklist
You need to develop your own checklist which is specific to your subject. This will help you to isolate more of the things which are causing difficulties for an individual pupil. **Checklist 3** in this book provides some initial ideas that might help you to do this. However, it needs to be re-interpreted and extended in the context of your own subject. **Begin this now.** You will need to extend and develop this list further as your experience of teaching continues to grow.

In using all three checklists it is very important to make a note of pupils' strengths as well as their difficulties. Knowing what a pupil can do *well* will give you guidance in planning the contexts in which provision can be made and the methods which are most likely to be successful.

Remember too that pupils who appear, in the course of normal lessons, to be having problems of a similar order, may have very different strengths and weaknesses. Diagnostic investigation of these is, therefore, of great importance, not as an academic exercise or merely as a way of writing a detailed report on the pupil, but as the basis for planning what provision is needed and how you will begin to make it.

Checklist 1
For pupils with subject-specific language difficulties

Name ——————————— Class ———————————

Subject ——————————— Date ———————————

Put a tick (and a comment) against any item that applies to this pupil. Remember to add notes about what a pupil is good at and what he/she can do.

References in the margin are to activities in this book which will help to overcome some of these difficulties.

1. Oral difficulties   **Chapter 5**
  a) Difficulty in sustaining attention/listening ——————————   Section 5.2

  (This can be the result of a general language difficulty or can simply indicate that the pupil does not understand the content.)

  b) Difficulty in using vocabulary of subject appropriately ——————   Section 5.3

2. Reading and understanding   **Chapter 6**

  a) Difficulty in extracting information from printed material e.g.

    i) asks for clarification from teachers/peers ——————————   Section 6.2/6.3

    ii) avoids use of textbooks ——————————————   Section 6.5b

    iii) finds using teacher-made worksheets difficult ——————   Section 6.5c

  b) Reading response apparently fluent but comprehension poor ————   Section 6.2

3. Writing   **Chapter 7**
  a) Difficulty in organising information ———————————   Section 7.3

  b) Difficulty in organising own ideas —————————————

4. Spelling
  Difficulty with subject specific vocabulary ————————————   Section 7.5

Checklist 2
For pupils with general language difficulties

Name _____ Class _____

Subject _____ Date _____

Put a tick (and a comment) against any item that applies to this pupil.
Remember to make a note of what the pupil is good at and *can do*.
Use the ideas in the sections indicated to support pupils with these kinds of
difficulties.

Chapter 5 Section 5.1	**1. Oral difficulties** a) Difficulty in following oral instructions _____
Section 5.2	b) Difficulty in sustaining attention/listening _____
Section 5.1	c) Difficulty in making self understood _____
Chapter 6	**2. Reading and Understanding**
Section 6.4	a) Reading response e.g.
	i) jerky, gets stuck frequently _____
	ii) halting, line by line _____
	iii) slow, with little sense of meaning _____
Section 6.4c	b) Difficulty in using printed material
	e.g. contents, index, library sources _____
Chapter 7 Section 7.4c	**3. Writing** a) Poorly formed handwriting _____
Section 7.4c	b) Rate of writing too slow or hurried _____
Section 7.4d	c) Cannot copy from blackboard _____
Section 7.4e	d) Confuses letters e.g. 'b' and 'd' _____
Section 7.5	**4. Spelling** Difficulty with common everyday words _____

Checklist 3

For pupils with learning difficulties in (Subject) _____

Name _____   Class _____

Teacher _____   Date _____

Put a tick (and a comment) against any item that applies to this pupil.
Remember to make a note of things the pupil is good at and *can* do.
References in the margin are to activities in this book which will help to
overcome some of these difficulties.

1. General cognitive difficulties
   a) Imprecise, unsystematic observation _____   **Chapter 3**
                                                                    Section 3.2a

   b) Difficulties with spatial reasoning _____   Section 3.2b

   c) Difficulties with time _____   Section 3.2c

   d) _____

   e) _____

2. Difficulties in numeracy/maths   **Chapter 4**
   a) Difficulties in *understanding* material presented mathematically_____   Sections 4.1, 4.2
                                                                          4.3a, 4.3b

   b) *Doing* maths in any subject _____   Sections 4.3c to 4.3g

3. Other difficulties related to your subject   **Chapter 3**
   a) Difficulty in learning new concepts _____   Section 3.2e

   b) _____

   c) _____

You need to develop all parts of this checklist by reference to a range of
subject-specific literature and through discussion with colleagues in school.

**If you are worried about pupils but they do not merit any comment on any one
of these lists ask yourself whether their difficulty is a behaviour problem rather
than a learning problem. They are not always easy to tell apart!**

These checklists will help you to diagnose the nature of the difficulty which a pupil has. In most cases they also refer you to appropriate sections of this book for guidance on ways in which you might help the pupil to overcome these difficulties. You will, of course, have to design subject-specific activities to help pupils with any of the extra difficulties that you have listed on Checklist 3.

Activity 2.2a

- Test out these activities with your pupils.

- Keep a record of anything that you try and note how successful it was.

- This will be important information if you need to seek more detailed advice on an individual pupil.

Remember that many of the strategies which are suggested throughout this book as ways of making special provision for a pupil who has difficulty in your class can also be applied to your work with the class as a whole. The ideas in Section 6.3, for example, can be very effectively used with pupils of all abilities to provide challenging and instructive lessons based on a piece of text. Try, from time to time, to incorporate some of these ideas into your normal lesson planning. By doing so you will be making a practical response to the concept that special needs are the result of an interaction between the characteristics of the pupils and the nature of the teaching to which they are exposed – and you may well find that you reduce the number of pupils who need further, more individual attention.

Thinking

3

3.1 The characteristics of pupils with learning difficulties

The first thing to say about pupils with learning difficulties is that they are much like other pupils. Effective methods for teaching them are developments of normal teaching. They are not entirely different, nor are they mysterious techniques which lie right outside the experience of the mainstream subject teacher (see the Bullock Report, (DES, 1975)). This applies even to pupils who are educated in special schools for, as Swann (1983) says, the kinds of teaching and learning activities which go on in there are often 'strikingly ordinary'. This has two implications for your own teaching: it suggests that you can do a great deal to help pupils with learning difficulties without having to acquire a completely different set of teaching skills, and it suggests that the developments that you make in your teaching when finding ways of helping such pupils, will often be relevant to your teaching of other pupils too.

Having first stressed this similarity, it is also, of course, useful to discuss some of the differences between pupils with learning difficulties and other pupils. Research conducted by cognitive psychologists, mostly in the last ten to fifteen years, is beginning to give some useful insights into these differences. This work tends to be focused on pupils with quite extensive difficulties, for instance those with IQs of the order of 75, who will be amongst the least able pupils in many mainstream schools. Examples of the more common findings are given in Figure 3.1.

Such research results can confirm, refine or add to the important insights that you will gain in your day-to-day work with pupils who have learning difficulties. Of course, as far as an individual pupil is concerned, any or even most of the results may be inapplicable, and even when you are thinking about learning difficulties in more general terms, the results do not *directly* tell you what to do. However, they can help you to reflect on your current practice and may give you some starting points for developing that practice.

It is especially interesting that the pupil difficulties such as those listed in Figure 3.1, while they may be implicated in a pupil's inability to read well, and may give clues as to how we might help a pupil overcome this particular difficulty, will also have profound effects on many other aspects of the pupil's work in school. Provision for pupils with learning difficulties, whether it is provision that you make in your classroom, or provision made by the special

Figure 3.1

Pupils with learning difficulties:

● may have poor memories, (they seem not to group things together nor to categorise things when trying to memorise them, and seem to make less effective use of strategies such as rehearsal);

● tend to be slow, not only in doing large-scale tasks such as solving a maths problem, but also in performing simple mental processes (e.g. searching their memory for a simple piece of information such as the name of the letter 'a');

● can easily be distracted by novel or irrelevant information in a problem;

● tend not to generalise from one situation to another;

● in problem-solving, are poor at identifying exactly what the problem is;

● tend not to generate problem-solving strategies of their own;

● make poor selections of problem-solving strategies that they may have available to them;

● are poor at monitoring their own attempts at problem-solving so that they can give appropriate amounts of time to different stages and so that they can sense 'dead ends';

● have difficulty with if-then relationships;

● tend to be imprecise, impulsive and non-systematic in collecting information, both from observation of the 'real world' or from books;

● and, of course, they tend to know less than other children, which is a result of their other difficulties, but may also contribute to the continued existence of these difficulties.

(Ashman, 1984; Sternberg, 1984; Campione et al, 1982)

needs department in a school, should not, therefore, be limited to help with reading and other literacy tasks. It is for this reason that in the later sections of this chapter, and in the two chapters to follow, we will offer some advice about support in areas other than literacy. When we turn to the question of literacy in Chapters 6 and 7, we will still draw attention to the relevance of research findings such as those in Figure 3.1 from time to time.

Activity 3.1 may help you to become more familiar with some of the basic problems faced by pupils with learning difficulties, and help you to see their relevance to the design of support for individual pupils.

Activity 3.1

1. Focus on a pupil who is having difficulty in learning in your lessons.

2. Consider his or her particular difficulties in the light of the list of points made in Figure 3.1.
   a) List any of these characteristics which apply to the pupil you are considering.
   b) What other similar characteristics are you aware of?

Most important

3. Make a note of the implications of your list of characteristics for your teaching of this pupil, e.g. what could you do to help the pupil become more systematic in observation?

4. Repeat the exercise for one or two other pupils.

5. Compare your ideas with the suggestions offered later in this chapter and elsewhere in this book.

This sort of creative thinking about some of the problems which are experienced by pupils with learning difficulties is a vital step in developing your classroom practice. However, it is also important, and encouraging (!), to take note of what they *can* achieve. In a stimulating book, Weber (1978) describes many examples of successful work with slow learners drawn from his own classroom experience. He describes their success in oral and listening tasks, in reading and writing, and in creative, logical and critical thinking. He also outlines the circumstances in which this success was achieved. Even the title of the book, *Yes, they can!,* indicates that failure is not inevitable for these pupils and that, for a thoughtful teacher, there is everything to play for.

One example of Weber's work was concerned with pupils in the IQ range 58–90. He found that these pupils were successful in working on their own to solve puzzles and problems under certain circumstances. These circumstances were:
   a) that the problems were presented orally rather than on paper;
   b) that they were presented to a group of pupils and discussed within the group until everyone was clear what each problem was;
   c) that the pupils were given relevant materials so that they could physically manipulate things to try out ideas for solving each problem; and
   d) that the problems were presented in a concrete context (e.g. moving sections of fence to build pens for cattle rather than moving lines to turn squares into triangles).

This example, alone, is rich in general ideas for teaching such pupils more effectively. However in the next section we will give advice about dealing with rather more specific difficulties.

3.2 Helping pupils with specific difficulties

In this section we will discuss a number of areas of normal school work which pupils with learning difficulties may find problematic. Literacy problems and mathematical difficulties will be dealt with in separate chapters and so will not be discussed here. Some of the areas of difficulty considered below may be matters of particularly high priority to the teaching of some subjects, but we feel that, in addition, they all have some application across a wide range of curriculum subjects.

a) Making observations

Here we are thinking of two major issues: making observations from direct experience of the world (e.g. in a science experiment, or French exchange, or geography or history field trip), and making observations from pictures, charts, graphs and the like in books. There is clearly a direct link between both of these activities and the finding reported in Figure 3.1 that pupils with learning difficulties tend to be imprecise, impulsive and non-systematic in making observations of both kinds.

A useful idea in encouraging a systematic approach to observation is given in Activity 3.2a.

Activity 3.2a

1. Give each pupil a pair of similar pictures such as those in a newspaper 'spot the difference' competition. At first keep most of the differences fairly clear but include one or two which are easier to miss and keep at least one of them away from the centre of interest in the picture.

2. Ask pupils to work individually to find the differences.

3. Then, in groups, get them to check their results and to talk to one another about how they scanned the picture to try to find the differences.

4. In a class discussion check answers against the full list of differences, and get the most successful pupils to explain how they did it.

5. Emphasise the characteristics of good strategies e.g.
    a) thinking in advance about the sorts of differences there might be (say in the size, shape, colour, pattern, orientation of parts of the picture);
    b) systematically scanning across the picture in horizontal bands and down the picture as each band follows below the one before;
    c) systematically scanning in bands running in a different direction (in case the context in one scanning pattern obscures some differences);
    d) going back over areas of fine detail (irrespective of whether they are the areas which seem most interesting).

This observation game can be repeated with more complex and more detailed pictures, and can be made more subject-specific by using material such as diagrams of scientific apparatus set up for an experiment, maps drawn at different times in the development of an area, or pictures in which many of the differences are in labels which are in a foreign language.

The important thing is that, through a fairly light-hearted game, pupils are learning some effective strategies for looking closely and non-impulsively at things. The explicit discussion of their strategies, and of what was good and bad about them, is therefore a very important part of the game. Another crucial point is that you take opportunities to remind pupils of these strategies in other situations where they need to observe something closely. Remember that they may not be very good at generalising what they have learnt and will probably need help to appreciate that the same sort of strategies would help them to be aware of, say, all the detail contained in a diagram in a maths question.

b) Spatial reasoning

Are pupils always aware that a symbol $\rightarrowtail\!\!\leftarrow$ on a map is the same as the symbol $)\,($ in the key and that both therefore represent a bridge? Similarly is the battery symbol $\dashv\!\vdash$ recognised as being the same as the symbol $\perp$?

Some pupils may need to be helped to see that in these sorts of case all that is happening is that the symbol is being rotated. One way of helping to establish this idea is to let pupils build up maps or circuit diagrams not by drawing (where the rotation of the elements is not immediately apparent) but by putting together the various symbols which have been drawn out on small pieces of card. Especially if they are asked to talk to you about what they are doing, they can then see that they are rotating the symbols as they move them around their map and that, in fact, these different patterns on the page are the same thing, rotated.

It is important to help pupils to generalise this knowledge, but not to over-generalise it. 'p' and 'd' are two different letters, *not* a symbol for some physical object that can be rotated and moved about just as the object itself can be rotated and moved about. Similarly '+' and '×' are codes for two different mathematical operations, they do not represent some physical object. These potential confusions should be brought into the open and discussed. The temptation not to mention them to 'avoid confusion' is to risk the possibility that pupils are quietly storing up trouble for themselves.

Pupils may also need help over the language of spatial reasoning. If you think this is unnecessary try to remember the knots we can all get into when asked for a complicated set of directions by a stranger to our home town. Pupils with learning difficulties may certainly need help to be secure in the use of 'left' 'right' 'in front' and 'behind' and to understand them as directions defined in relation to their own body or to that of some specified person, on the street, in a picture or on a map. They also need help to recognise that 'north' 'south' 'east' and 'west' are not defined like this and do not work in the same way. In Section 5.1 we describe a map game which can be used to encourage talking and listening abilities. It can be played in two ways – using 'left' and 'right' directions or using compass directions. If you want to help pupils to sort out these two systems of talking about spatial relations, get them to play both versions of the game one after the other and to talk with you about the different ways in which the directions work. (For instance, you

See Section 5.1 page 30

turn north to get to Birmingham whether you are travelling from London to Gloucester or from Gloucester to London, but you turn left travelling from Gloucester to London and right travelling from London to Gloucester.)

c) Time

A proper understanding of time is important in many aspects of school life. It is simple to recognise that it affects individuals' ability to manage their day-to-day life so that they get to places on time and allow themselves sufficient time to do things. One can also readily accept that an understanding of time is important to academic work in history, in the sciences (through concepts such as velocity and acceleration and through notions of rate of change) and in any other subject which uses these concepts. However, the need to understand how time 'works' is more pervasive than this. The temporal ordering of events is closely linked to explanations of cause and effect. If A comes before B it *could* be a cause of B, but if A comes after B it cannot. Pupils would have difficulty with time may therefore find themselves with difficulties in situations where the involvement of temporal notions is by no means obvious.

This widespread effect of difficulties with ideas of time is especially important because time tends to be problematic for pupils with learning difficulties. It is easy to see why this should be so. First the ideas of time are abstract. Secondly, to make sense of temporal arguments, the pupil needs to be able to look at a situation from another person's point of view. For example, a pupil needs to be able to recognise that for a person in 1950, 1970 was in the future. Both of these aspects of time, if viewed from the perspective of Piaget's work, lead us to expect that ideas related to time will be confusing for pupils with learning difficulties.

One step in helping pupils who have difficulty with time is to check that they know the relationship between different units. For example you might ask them to say whether 30 seconds is equal to, more than, or less than half a minute; whether a year is equal to, more than, or less than 36 months. Another useful step is the sorting task described in Activity 3.2c.

Activity 3.2c
Sorting task

1. Give to each pair of pupils four or five pictures which make up a clear temporal sequence. At first choose sequences which are very familiar such as the build up of clouds leading to rain and to the formation of puddles.

2. Get them to sort them into the right order, talking to one another (and to you) about their reasoning for one order rather than another. The ideas of cause and effect and their relation to the time sequence will emerge from such discussion.

3. Place the pictures in the right order on an appropriate 'time line'. For the weather example an appropriate line might be

   | 10.00 | 10.15 | 10.30 | 10.45 | 11.00 |

4. Repeat the game with other sequences which take place over shorter or longer periods to build up the idea of time lines with very different scales.

The time line, once established as a way of recording the relationship of events in time can be very useful for visualising such relationships in all sorts of time-dependent processes, on all sorts of scales including the historical or geological. Ideas of 'before' and 'after', and of 'past', 'present' and 'future' can all be discussed by reference to the more concrete ideas of left and right on the time line. The importance of recognising different points of view – for instance, the earlier example of 1970 being 'future' for a person in 1950 – can also be discussed in these more concrete terms.

d) A source of further ideas

The ideas in Sections a) to c) above owe much to the work of Feuerstein, and in particular to his 'Instrumental Enrichment' programme (Feuerstein et al, 1980). This seeks to improve pupils' basic abilities in tasks such as observing, comparing, categorising, giving and following instructions, and understanding spatial, temporal and numerical relationships. It seeks to improve pupils' ability to reason logically and plan solutions to problems. It is designed to help pupils acquire basic concepts and the language of reasoning, and seeks to develop in pupils the habit of reflecting on a problem rather than, impulsively, grabbing at an answer. It seeks to improve pupils' motivation for problem solving and to improve their self-image as effective solvers of problems and active participants in their own learning.

Instrumental Enrichment (IE) makes use of some 500 pencil and paper exercises which are designed to improve pupils' functioning in the areas of observing, comparing etc, as listed above. These are not based on normal curriculum content, but are described as 'content free'. In a typical IE lesson, pupils work individually on these 'instruments' for about 30 minutes, with individual help from the teacher as necessary. This work is preceded by an introductory discussion and followed by a time when the pupils and their teacher, as a group, talk about the strategies that they used, review the concepts and vocabulary that were involved, evaluate different ways of tackling the problems and make links between the IE task and relevant parts of the mainstream curriculum, and between the IE task and general problem solving in day-to-day life outside school. This brief description does nothing to reveal the theoretical structure behind the IE programme, nor does it do justice to the programme itself, however it may encourage you to find out more. This might be done through the literature which we have quoted in this section. However, several LEAs in Britain have arranged for teachers to be trained in the use of Instrumental Enrichment. You might therefore be able to get some specialist advice on, and practical experience of, the programme from someone in your own school or LEA.

Formal evaluations of the programme are still scarce, and those that exist are somewhat contradictory. Blackman and Lin (1984) are guarded in their assessment of the effectiveness of Instrumental Enrichment, though their main concern is with its effectiveness with pupils who have quite severe learning difficulties. They argue that the evaluations which have been done to date have not included sufficient numbers of such pupils for clear conclusions to be drawn about their response to IE. They seem particularly unconvinced of the extent to which the effects of the IE programme are generalised by such pupils to their other school work. However, Arbitman-Smith and colleagues (1984), writing of a broader group of pupils with learning difficulties, present more positive findings which they summarise as follows:

In general the results are encouraging but not overwhelming. For example, after 1 year of IE, students commonly show gains of 5–10 IQ points; gains

are found on some standardised achievement tests but not in all areas. By contrast, more marked changes in classroom learning behaviour and in enthusiasm for learning are commonly observed...

Although the effects of IE are not absolutely clear cut, these changes in learning behaviour and in enthusiasm could pave the way for successful learning, especially if other aspects of the teaching of a pupil with special educational needs were sensitive to his or her difficulties. Alternatively, the ideas of IE could be incorporated into normal subject teaching by working in the IE style on 'instruments' derived more closely from normal subject content. Either way, it would seem to be well worth exploring the IE programme in some detail so that its ideas could be allowed to influence creative thought about improving the education of pupils who have difficulty in learning.

e) Concepts

A fascinating question for all teachers in secondary schools is how to help pupils, and especially pupils with learning difficulties, to acquire and to use the often complex, usually abstract concepts which are fundamental to an understanding of their subject.

Undoubtedly an important starting point is the pupils' own preconceived ideas of what might be the explanation of situations in which any given concept applies. For example, many pupils have difficulty in appreciating the importance of the concept of density in explaining why some things float and some sink. If a pupil's preconceived notion is simply that wood floats because it is wood, and metal sinks because it is metal, then the teacher's attempt to bring the difficult idea of density into play will seem to be mysterious, unnecessary and a typical example of teachers making something that is simple seem hard! What is more, since common experience would offer no challenges to the pupil's ideas, there would be no stimulus to abandon the simple explanation and adopt the teacher's more complex one.

Two ideas emerge from this paragraph.

First, we need to know what pupils' preconceived notions are. Some general ideas can be obtained from research results. To continue with a scientific example, Simpson and Arnold (1982) reported that 44 per cent of pupils aged 14+ thought that carbon and carbohydrates were gases. General results of this kind can alert us to the kinds of misconception which are likely to be interfering with the learning of pupils with difficulties. However, it may well be that such pupils have particularly idiosyncratic preconceived ideas. It is, therefore, important not to rely entirely on general studies of this kind for insights into pupils' starting points, but to try to find out from individual pupils themselves what they think about a problem under investigation in class. Two ways of trying to do this are to look closely at the *kinds* of errors which pupils are making in their written work (rather than concentrating on the *number* of errors so as to give a mark out of ten), and to listen and respond sensitively to what pupils say when they discuss the problem with you and with their peers.

Secondly, having identified these misconceptions, we should try to provide some experience which will challenge what the pupil thinks. In the flotation example, we might ask the pupil to try floating a dense piece of wood on alcohol, when it sinks, or to watch as we float a piece of metal on mercury, when it floats. By exposing a shortcoming in their own 'explanation' of floating we provide the stimulus for them to be more open minded which then at least gives a starting point for introducing the generally accepted ideas. Nussbaum and Norvick (1981) describe this sort of procedure at some length and suggest that it is quite successful.

Other ideas for helping pupils to acquire concepts include giving lots of examples of the concept so that pupils' views of it are not inappropriately narrowed by the examples they meet, and giving lots of non-examples so that pupils learn the limits of the concept and are not over-inclusive. Another important idea is to draw attention to possibly confusing concepts so that the differences between them can deliberately be brought to pupils' attention. It can also be helpful if similar concepts are taught in different ways. Energy and momentum, for example, are easily confused when pupils first begin to use them. This confusion is probably not reduced by the fact that both concepts tend to be taught using the same apparatus, such as trolley boards and ticker timers.

Finally, it is important to note that relatively little research has been done on the acquisition of the sorts of concept that we have been discussing in this section. The ideas suggested should therefore be taken up in a spirit of enquiry. Like many of the other ideas in this chapter, they are not prescriptions of teaching methods that *will* work, but suggestions for methods that might work; they are ideas that are worth investigating in your own context with your own pupils; they are ideas that you will want to develop, not follow slavishly.

4

Difficulties in numeracy and mathematics

4.1 Introduction

There can be little doubt that number, and other aspects of mathematics, cause difficulties for some pupils, not only in their maths classes but almost universally throughout the secondary school curriculum. It is easy to see that this is the case if we compare survey results on what pupils find difficult in maths with the demands which we are likely to make on pupils in our normal teaching. For example the Cockcroft Report (DES, 1982) points out that there is a 'seven year difference in achieving an understanding of place value which is sufficient to write down the number which is 1 more than 6399'. Some pupils can do this at age seven; others cannot do it even at the age of fourteen.

Similarly, the APU reports (APU, 1981,1982) make it clear that 22 per cent of 15 year olds had difficulty with decimal place value and responded to questions as if the decimal point was not there. These reports also showed that some 10 per cent of 15 year olds had difficulty with addition, that between 10 per cent and 20 per cent had difficulty with subtraction and that these figures increased when the numbers that had to be manipulated in a problem were presented in some form other than vertical columns. APU showed that at least 20 per cent of pupils had difficulties with ratio and proportion and that this figure varied with the context of the question and with the awkwardness of the numbers involved in the calculation. Indeed, for one question it reached 80 per cent.

Many subjects in the secondary curriculum make at least some use of such basic mathematical ideas and operations. An historian will talk about the percentage of people employed on the land in 1800. A geographer will discuss scales on a map. Even in modern language lessons we may ask pupils to work out costs from a menu or journey times from a timetable written in the foreign language. In almost any subject we might discuss a topic such as unemployment which demands some understanding of mathematical issues if pupils are to make sense of the numerical trends which are often at the crux of the argument. However, do we usually consider the *mathematical* demands which we are making in such lessons? Do we think about the way in which pupils can appreciate the historical or geographical concepts involved in studying changes in land use, if they have difficulty with the idea of percentage in which the raw data are expressed.

The difficulty is even greater in some subjects (notably the sciences) which make much more extensive use of mathematical concepts. This is clearly demonstrated by other findings from the APU surveys. These showed, for example, that between 10 and 25 per cent of pupils had difficulty with the use of indices, often using them simply as multipliers. Also many pupils had difficulty substituting numbers into an equation. In substituting numbers into the equation $v = u + gt$, even when using a calculator to do the arithmetic, 25 per cent of pupils simply added u, g and t. Well over 25 per cent found it hard to simplify algebraic expressions, and 20 per cent had difficulties comparing the size of angles.

A full study of the APU reports would reveal more detail of this kind. However, what has already been said is enough to indicate that pupils with general learning difficulties may well have specific difficulty with the mathematical content of their lessons across the curriculum as a whole. Other pupils who cope perfectly well with the literacy demands and general demands of lessons may also have difficulties with mathematical ideas. Whatever subject we teach, we should therefore be alert to the mathematical demands of our lessons, and the difficulties which these might create.

Activity 4.1
Think about your last five lessons with one class.

1. What mathematical demands did you make?
a) Did you ask the pupils to use any sort of measuring instrument? Did this involve a decimal scale (as when they are asked to measure a length of 2.3cm)?
b) Did you talk about time intervals or distances which would involve subtraction?
c) Did pupils use graphs or tables or histograms?
d) Did they use ideas of area or volume?
e) Did you talk about ratio or proportion (perhaps implicitly, by discussing density or speed)?

These tasks all make basic mathematical demands on the pupil. So do many others.

2. Were there more advanced mathematical demands e.g. indices, formulae, equations, algebra, others?

3. What did you do in each case to help pupils who found the maths (rather than the history or science) difficult?

Often, the mathematical demands made by a lesson will not be obvious to you unless you force yourself to think about it by an activity such as Activity 4.1. Even more often you may choose not to, or forget to, make them explicit to your pupils. This may be because you are not very confident about maths yourself, and hope that the pupils will cope with the maths demands of the lesson without any intervention on your part. It may also be because advice on how to support pupils with mathematical difficulties is less widespread than advice in other major areas of special needs, especially the area of literacy. Unfortunately, the pupil who is given limited maths support in your mainstream lessons is also likely to receive rather limited maths support outside your classroom (e.g. from special needs staff). The Cockcroft Report, for example, revealed an imbalance between the amounts of attention given to literacy and numeracy in schools.

There can be no doubt, therefore, that mathematical difficulties must be the concern of all teachers. The rest of this chapter makes some suggestions about how to offer support.

4.2 Who has what difficulties in mathematics?

In parallel with reading test data, secondary schools will often have a record of pupils' scores on a standardised maths test. These can give some initial clues to pupils who are likely to have difficulty with the mathematical demands of your lessons. Also, as you assess your pupils' normal work, you can be alert to the possibility that mistakes on your subject content may sometimes be a result of a mathematical difficulty. Therefore, you can also help to identify the pupils who have problems of this kind.

These identification procedures do not usually give many clues about the nature of the difficulty which the pupil has. Some of the common maths screening tests are not designed to give information of this kind, and even where others can provide diagnostic information, for example in the case of the NFER Basic Mathematics Tests, scores are often reported in a way that prevents them from being used for this purpose.

One way of gaining diagnostic insights is to look for patterns of error in everyday work. Particularly where a pupil has had time to consider his or her answers, consistent mistakes, for instance ignoring the decimal point in a number of different calculations, can give useful clues to the kinds of difficulty which the pupil has (Bentley and Malvern, 1983). Another approach is to ask questions which are specifically designed to expose misunderstandings (Rees and Barr, 1983). Such questions have to be carefully chosen. The examples below, adapted from Rees and Barr, illustrate this point: 0.2×0.2 (which is often thought to be 0.4) will show up a difficulty with decimal place value whereas 0.4×0.4 may be answered correctly despite considerable misunderstanding on this point; $1/x=3/4$ will require true algebraic reasoning and will reveal errors in that reasoning whereas $2/x=1/4$ can be solved by just trying out some numbers to see if one works and may therefore conceal the pupil's difficulty. Valuable diagnostic information can also be gained by listening to pupils talk their way through a mathematical problem in your subject. This can give a great deal of insight, in a relatively short time, into faulty strategies that a pupil has adopted to solve problems. Finally, tests designed for diagnostic use can be given. One interesting example is the Chelsea Diagnostic Mathematics Test published by NFER.

It is unlikely, if you are not a mathematician, that you will get very closely involved in these kinds of diagnostic assessment of pupils' maths difficulties. However, some awareness of what can be done may be useful. You would then know that you might need to seek advice about a pupil who seems to get into trouble with the more mathematical parts of your subject. You would also be aware of the kinds of information you could ask for from the maths or special needs staff.

4.3 Some strategies for helping pupils

a) Consistency

A major issue is consistency from teacher to teacher in the language that is used to talk about maths. The need to consider this point is immediately apparent if you ask a group of colleagues to read out $4.01x(2x+3)^2$. A variety of perfectly correct readings will undoubtedly emerge. This kind of variety, from lesson to lesson, in the way in which teachers talk about maths is certain to add to any confusion felt by a pupil who has difficulty with mathematical ideas.

Of similar importance is consistency over the use of letters in formulae and equations. If mathematicians use $F=ma$ and physicists use $p=mf$ to stand for exactly the same relationship, then it is hardly surprising if pupils are confused and fail to see that one subject is of relevance to the other.

Activity 4.3a

1. Find out how your colleagues in the maths department and the special needs department 'talk maths' to pupils.

2. Find out what letter conventions colleagues use.

3. Find out how colleagues write abbreviations for units (m/s, ms^{-1} etc).

4. Avoid inconsistencies wherever possible. If there is some very good reason for using different terminology make sure you bring the different usage to the attention of your pupils so that they know that the same thing is being talked about in different ways.

b) Language

The language you use in talking about the mathematical parts of any lesson should be thought about with great care. One reason why this is an important issue is that an APU report (1982a; Para 7.3) has revealed that even small changes in the way in which a problem is phrased can significantly affect the difficulty which pupils will have with it. Secondly, teachers' language to pupils tends to be more complex when talking about a maths problem than when discussing other areas of the curriculum. Finally, mathematics uses common words in very specific ways. For example 'volume' may mean a knob on their music centres to pupils, 'area' may mean the part of the town where they live, and discussion of 'vulgar fractions' may conjure up all sorts of unpleasant expectations!

All these points suggest that you should think very carefully about the language that you use when you are discussing mathematical ideas. They are considered at greater length in Bentley and Malvern (1983, pp 7–9).

The importance of the question of language can be further illustrated by taking an example from history lessons. If we read 1930 as 'nineteen thirty' and 1986 as 'nineteen eighty six' will the pupils immediately recognise that they can manipulate those dates in the same way that they can manipulate the numbers 'one thousand nine hundred and thirty' and 'one thousand nine hundred and eighty six'? For example will they see that they can subtract one from the other to find the time interval? A brief mention of the equivalence of the two conventional ways of saying the numbers might avoid much confusion.

Finally, remember that whether written or spoken, a *verbal* presentation of an idea involving mathematical concepts may not be the best approach. Where the idea of ratio is involved in teaching about land use, a pie chart may be a far more effective way of helping pupils to understand the information than a passage which states that 10 per cent of land was waste, 20 per cent was used for private dwellings etc.

c) Calculators

Even if the mathematical operation that is required in a particular piece of physics or geography is fairly straightforward, a simple division for example, the actual problem may be difficult for a pupil because the numbers are 'awkward'. This is especially likely if the numbers have come from an experiment or from distances measured from a map where it is not always possible to ensure that simple numbers emerge. These are ideal circumstances for the use of a calculator.

Some useful points to bear in mind are:

● that a pupil with significant difficulties over place value may have trouble entering numbers, – 'one thousand one hundred and two' might be entered as 10001002 rather than 1102;

● that pupils should be encouraged to make a rough estimate of the right answer before using the calculator so that keying errors can be detected and so that the exercise does not become 'mechanistic button pressing' (Williams, 1985);

● that there is evidence that the use of calculators does not produce any 'adverse effect on basic computational skill' (DES, 1982; Para 377) so you will not be undoing any basic skills work that may be done with the pupil by other staff.

● that some pupils may need help in interpreting answers that include a decimal point.

d) Talking through mathematical components of a lesson

Teacher talk

When a problem is written out in a maths or science book, there is a simple neat progression of ideas from the original question to the answer. Every step is productive: it leads on to the final solution. There are no loose ends or false starts. There is no clue to *why* the author chose to start the solution in a given way. There is no sense of the sort of struggle that is involved in finding a neat route to a solution (Kerslake, 1982).

This may well be appropriate for most examples of problem-solving in text books. However, when working through a problem with a group of pupils or with the whole class you might, with advantage, make your process of problem-solving much more explicit. This would involve being alert to the alternatives which might occur to pupils at each step and arguing out why the chosen alternative is the best, or the only, one worth pursuing.

Teacher-pupil and pupil-pupil talk

You should try to arrange for pupils to work together in groups to discuss their solutions to mathematical parts of your lessons. By talking about a problem, rather than having to commit themselves immediately to writing out an answer on their own, pupils may be prepared to try out ideas, offer partial solutions, and make rough approximations. By doing so they may talk

themselves into understanding. It can be particularly productive if you arrange to be involved in such sessions, listening at least as much as talking, so that you get a clearer picture of the difficulties the pupils are having.

e) Maths practicals

If you want the class to become familiar with a relationship between variables (such as the Ohm's Law relationship between voltage, current and resistance) get them to try out some numbers to see how the relationship works. For example, ask them to explore the equation $V/I = R$ and see what values they get for R for different values of V and I that they choose for themselves. This should be done in groups, almost certainly using calculators or a computer. When you discuss the results with them it should be possible to highlight the fact that large values of R emerge when a large voltage is associated with a small current. If ideas of voltage and current are already established, the concept of R being a 'resistance' to the flow of current should then 'make sense'. This can give pupils increased confidence in the use of the Ohm's Law equation by making it far less mysterious, and this in turn might help to demystify equations generally.

f) Giving hints and correcting errors

Kerslake (1982) argues that maths is an area in which answers are often either right or wrong. You therefore need to have a number of strategies available to you for helping pupils to avoid errors, and for correcting errors, so that you are not continually giving them the discouraging response that they are 'wrong'. Quoting Alan Bishop, Kerslake makes six suggestions: you can jog pupils' memories ('Don't forget the decimal point.'); you can show that their approach would lead to a silly answer so that *they* can tell *you* that they must be wrong; you can get them to think again about what they are trying to do in tackling the problem; you can offer some intermediate step in the solution; you can encourage them ('This one's hard isn't it.' 'Think again here.'); you can simply correct the mistake. Another approach might be to ask 'How did you get that answer?'

All these strategies can help. Try not to limit yourself to just one.

g) Some other ideas

If a lesson has a substantial maths content it may be possible to introduce the ideas in a qualitative way first, and then to add the mathematical element later. This might give the pupils a general 'feel' for the ideas which is useful in generating understanding of the subject content with which you are concerned. It may also give pupils the confidence to persevere with the maths when you begin to introduce it.

As mentioned earlier, draw explicit attention to the mathematical content of anything you ask the pupils to do. For example, explain to pupils how to set up axes for a graph. Point out the ideas and computational steps involved and discuss a sequence of steps that will enable them to do the task successfully.

Finally, another idea offered by Kerslake (1982) is of considerable value. She points out that it is important to help pupils cope with the symbols used in maths by getting them to verbalise what they see on the page. For example, the equation $y = 3x + 5$ can be easily solved once it is verbalised as 'multiply the value of x by 3. Add 5 to your answer. y is equal to that final result.'

Sometimes different ways of verbalising the same symbols help to make the problem simpler. 10/2 can be verbalised as '10 shared between 2 people'. However, $10/\frac{1}{2}$ is best verbalised as 'How many halves are there in 10?' – '10 shared between $\frac{1}{2}$ a person' does not help much! Therefore encourage pupils to think of more than one way of reading the symbols.

4.4 Summary

One major advantage of having a range of strategies available to help pupils with the maths content of your lessons is that they will be more successful in coping with your subject. Another substantial advantage is that you can play your part in weakening the image of maths as something that is frightening, something which is only accessible to certain people such as whiz kid pupils and maths teachers, and something which has no relevance outside maths lessons. Any progress in these directions will be of considerable benefit to pupils in their day-to-day life in a society which communicates many important ideas through the medium of number.

Talking and listening

5

5.1 Introduction

The main purpose in helping pupils with difficulties in this area is to enable them to become more effective communicators in the classroom, to be better at listening and at talking. There are many ways of developing this in pupils, and we suggest some below. An important general point is that we frequently do not give our pupils enough *time* to express themselves in busy classrooms. Remember too that some pupils may find it easier to listen and talk in small groups or when they are on their own in conversation with you. Therefore, it is important during your lessons to organise a variety of contexts for talking and listening on the part of the pupils.

If pupils have difficulty in following instructions remember to repeat what you have said in another way, or speak to those particular pupils again privately as the others get down to work and you are free to move round the room. Remember to find as many different ways as possible to give the same instructions and, above all, give pupils enough time for what they want to say. Remember to allow pupils the opportunity to make use of their own relevant real experience to illustrate a point you are making. Ask for volunteers who can think of examples in their own lives of the points which you are making in class.

Specific ways of developing effective communication include many activities with which you are already familiar. See, for instance, Activity 5.1a.

Activity 5.1a
When you are planning some group work, brief one pupil from each group while other pupils get out books and equipment. This encourages pupils to give instructions to each other.

Another general strategy that can be useful is given in Activity 5.1b.

An example of a rather more explicit activity designed to improve listening and talking ability is given in Activity 5.1c on the next page.

In Chapter 3, we discussed two ways of playing this map game to improve pupils' use and understanding of the vocabulary of spatial reasoning. You might find it helpful to look back to this chapter at this point.

See Section 3.2b, page 15.

Activity 5.1b
Arrange your preliminary work on a topic so that groups of pupils have different kinds of information which they need to pool in order to carry out the project you have in mind. When this preliminary work has been completed get someone from each group to present their set of results. In choosing pupils for this you must make sure that it is not always the most articulate and fluent talkers who take on this role of reporter. The first time you try this pupils may not be good at it, but they can learn to be successful communicators and it is worth perservering.

Activity 5.1c
Map game
(This requires some preparation on your part but is valuable in developing pupils' communication skills.)

1. Have two copies of a town map: one which shows only roads, and another which includes labelled buildings.

2. Place two pupils opposite each other with a shield between them so that neither can see the other's map (an open book will do).

3. The one with the map showing buildings has to direct the other from, for instance, the railway station to the church. This is achieved by describing where the railway station is and then directing the other participant along different roads to the church.

4. When the game is completed, remove the shield and compare the two maps – perhaps they will need to discuss what went wrong and then have another go!

A wide range of further ideas for talking and listening games is provided by Weber (1978). Two further suggestions are given in Activities 5.1d and 5.1e.

Activity 5.1d
Cardigan Game

- Ask a pair of pupils to do the task, making sure there is at least one cardigan for the pair.
- One pupil instructs the other on how to put on a cardigan. The second pupil is required to do whatever the first pupil says with respect to putting on the cardigan.

This activity may be done most effectively by two pupils in front of the class as a means of indicating the pitfalls and dilemmas which are inevitable in giving and receiving purely verbal instructions. It could be used as a priming activity with the whole class, before setting the pupils to work in pairs on the map game. Also, if the activity was tape recorded, a transcript could be worked on by pupils in pairs to develop a 'correct' set of instructions. These might themselves be tried out with some amusement!

Activity 5.1e
Alphabet Games

1. Each pupil says a word in turn. The first letter of the first word has to be 'a', the first letter of the second word 'b' and so on.

2. Each pupil says a word which begins with the last letter of the previous word.

3. Each pupil says a sentence. This must begin with the letter which is next in the alphabet to that which began the last sentence. The sentences must follow on logically.

In these alphabet games each pupil has to both listen and talk. Both abilities are being exercised at the same time.

These activities can sensitise pupils to the difficulties of listening and talking accurately and can give them practice at improving these skills in a fairly lighthearted way. It can also be useful to design tasks which improve pupils' abilities to extract information from spoken material, (e.g. a text read out by the teacher) which has a subject-specific content. This can reinforce pupils' learning of subject-specific vocabulary and help poor readers to engage in study of a text which they might have difficulty in reading for themselves. Some ideas for such tasks are given in Activity 5.1f.

Activity 5.1f

1. One useful idea is a completion exercise.
   a) You read out a text and leave out a word or phrase.
   b) Stop reading at the end of the sentence from which the deletion was made.
   c) Pupils then try to supply missing text and discuss their ideas in small groups.

This activity is useful if the text contains subject-specific vocabulary, for pupils can be encouraged to think about the meaning of technical terms using clues from the surrounding text at the same time as they are learning to be more careful about the way in which they listen to speech which is intended to convey information.

2. A similar idea is to stop speaking before the end of the text and ask pupils to complete it. After they have had time to work on their version, you can continue reading the text aloud so that they can check their predictions. Mismatches should then be discussed to decide whether they are appropriate completions and, if not, to try to see where misunderstandings have crept in.

3. Another variation is to read aloud four paragraphs out of order. It is hard to put all four into order, but pupils might be asked to say which was the first, or the last, of the normal sequence.

4. Finally, pupils might be asked to jot down specific things as you read a text. They might, for example, jot down all the evidence for a given point of view if the aim is to analyse the text for bias or for attitudes.

All these tasks help pupils to extract information from speech. This is relevant in everyday life, whether listening to the radio or taking messages over the telephone and it is an important skill in school for pupils who have to listen to a great deal of exposition from teachers in the course of a year. They need the skills developed by these activities. And there is also the further pay-off that we have mentioned already, namely that through these Activities Relatd to Talk (ARTs) poor readers can begin to analyse text without being handicapped by their reading difficulties.

5.2 Poor concentration

There are several reasons for poor concentration. For instance pupils may lack interest in the lesson because they do not have any background information about the lesson topic, or they find your presentation difficult to follow. If children are lacking concentration Activity 5.2a may be useful.

Activity 5.2a
Ask yourself:

1. What is the necessary background for this piece of work?

2. Do pupils have it?
   (E.g. they need to understand the concepts of liquid and solids before you introduce the idea of dissolving.)
   Find this out by questioning, discussion, or a written test.
   Don't make assumptions.

3. Is there variety in the tasks they have to do?

4. Is there variety in the pace of the lesson?

5. Are the instructions clear?

Taking account of such things may help to improve the pupils' ability to concentrate in your lessons. However, levels of concentration will move between sharp focus on a topic and a more general level of awareness. This means that you will need to make sure that you mention each significant point more than once. Therefore, find several ways of introducing the same material and restate those pieces of information that you want to be sure your pupils will remember.

Frequently environmental factors can make pupils lethargic or uncooperative, sleepy or irritable. You should therefore always check the ventilation, heating and lighting in your classroom. It is particularly easy for conditions to become unconducive to work without your noticing if you have been working in one room for a whole afternoon, say, without stepping outside. It can be a real shock to come back into such a room after a brief time in the corridor or outside the building, and to realise just how unpleasant the conditions are in which you, and the pupils, have been trying to work.

Lack of concentration on the part of an individual pupil may also be provoked by physical difficulties like hearing loss or by other medical conditions or their treatment. See Activity 5.2b.

Activity 5.2b
Check the school records for those pupils who have physical difficulties.

If they have hearing loss, make sure that they sit near the front of the class or that you always move near to them when you are talking. Also be sure to face them when you are talking as they may supplement their poor hearing by attending to your lip movements. For similar reasons do not talk to the class with your back to the window: you will appear as a silhouette.

If they have other medical conditions and you suspect that lack of concentration is being caused by the condition or the drugs used to treat it, take steps to contact the school doctor for general advice (perhaps through a senior member of staff), or the pupil's GP (perhaps through his or her form tutor and parents). It may be that the timing or type of treatment can be adjusted to reduce these difficulties during the school day. Doctors are often very grateful for feedback on the effects of treatment regimes and may be willing to consider such changes. Clearly, parents should be involved in any contact with medical services about the specific treatment given to their child.

5.3 Subject-specific vocabulary

Using vocabulary that is specific to a subject needs plenty of encouragement and practice, as well as numerous examples and illustrations of what the words mean. Many subject-specific words have common use in the language too, and this can confuse some pupils (e.g. volume, space, function, mapping, etc).

Activity 5.3
When pupils participate in the lesson encourage them to use new words with associated examples and illustrations of what they mean. This will help you to pick up any misunderstandings early on.

Remember that the difficulty that pupils might have with subject-specific vocabulary may well be caused by their lack of understanding of the ideas as much as by their difficulty with the language itself.

Reading and understanding

6

6.1 Introduction

The reading that pupils do in school is a valuable extension of the work done orally with the classroom teacher. However, recent research (Lunzer and Gardner, 1979) has highlighted the actual use of text books in lesson and homework time. They observed that most reading in class time was of the 'short burst' variety, lasting between 15 and 30 seconds, and that a reading homework was viewed by pupils as a 'soft' option. Even when pupils did the reading set by their teacher, little learning took place because there was no structure to the activity or support of any other kind.

Learning from reading is not easy without help. It requires the reader to focus on parts of the text, reflect on and consider the meaning before taking in more information. It is essentially a *thoughtful* activity. Thoughtful reading presupposes a reading style quite unlike the 'smooth' reading of a novel, which can be described as a comparatively even flow of the eyes over the print. The reader needs to learn how to interrogate the text, stop and think while reading, and view their own experience in terms of that of the author.

In order to create the possibility of thinking while reading the activity itself needs to be interrupted in some way. Activities which can foster this 'broken' style of reading have been developed and described in further work by Lunzer and Gardner (1984). These activities are known as **D**irected **A**ctivities **R**elated to **T**ext (DARTs). They are briefly described below, after a general introduction to the basic ideas and to the practical requirements for their implementation.

6.2 Learning from reading – general points

Before setting a task involving learning from reading, you should consider the following points:

1. Is the reading material too easy or too difficult? (See Section 6.5) If the text is difficult it may still be possible to use it effectively, but only with considerable oral introduction and discussion before the pupils read it for themselves.

2. What background information will the pupils need in order to understand the text? Do they have this? If not, how are you going to provide them with this background. Remember that pupils with learning difficulties are likely to know less than other pupils – see Figure 3.1 (page 12).

3. Do any of the subject-specific vocabulary items require definition, explanation or discussion before the pupils read the text?

4. Does the text include sufficient information for the pupils to make their own summaries later? Is the passage sufficiently coherent for it to make sense to them as a complete unit of information?

5. It is always necessary for *you* to know beforehand what you want your pupils to understand as a result of their reading. Make sure that *they* also know exactly what you are expecting them to do with the text, and what the purpose of their reading is on any occasion.

Even when you have taken these things into account, some pupils may still have difficulty learning from their reading. There are various things which you can do to help further.

First it is important to get the pupils to engage in some sort of *interaction with the text* (for instance, underlining, labelling, sequencing, text completion and so on). These activities focus attention on the text, and provide explicit strategies for working with it. In this way they support pupils who have some of the difficulties that we outlined in Figure 3.1 (page 12).

Because of the memory problems of many pupils with learning difficulties (see Figure 3.1), to ensure that information obtained by reading is retained, pupils will need opportunities for *associated oral work*. This is best achieved by having groups of pupils working together on the activity you provide, allowing discussion to explore and shape the learning. You may sometimes wish to group the pupils in your class by reading ability and provide texts of different kinds for the different groups. Hopefully, whether you teach streamed or mixed ability classes, you will also use mixed ability groups within your class from time to time. In such groups the less able reader can take part with the more able pupil in the meaning-making discussion and argument that will be fostered.

Finally pupils will need the chance to crystallise their understanding through *writing*.

We will discuss these points in more detail below.

6.3 Directed Activities Related to Texts – DARTS

Figure 6.3

1. Pupils can be helped to prepare for reading by
  a) giving them structured over-views of the text
  b) checking that they understand specific vocabulary
  c) helping them to underline and label main ideas

2. Pupils can be helped to think through reading by
  a) completion tasks
  b) sequencing tasks
  c) prediction tasks
  d) diagram and table completion tasks

3. Pupils can be helped to consolidate their learning from reading by both oral discussion and writing

Section 2.1
Section 6.3a

Section 6.3b
Section 6.3c
Section 6.3d
Section 6.3e

Section 6.3f

This section discusses ways of doing the text-related activities mentioned in Figure 6.3.

a) Marking of texts – underlining and labelling

The technique of marking a passage helps to focus pupils' attention on the main ideas and helps them to appreciate those parts of the text which can be ignored for this purpose. See Activity 6.3a.

Activity 6.3a

1. Select an appropriate passage and photocopy sufficient copies for the class.
(Before photocopying remember to write to the publisher for permission. This is generally straightforward if you are clear about the passage you want to use and the purpose for which you want to use it.)

2. Have pupils work in pairs or small groups.

3. Invite them to underline or highlight the points in the text relevant to the purpose of your lesson. Different sorts of point (characteristics and motivations of a character in a history text, say) can be underlined in different colours.

or

4. Ask pupils to write labels on slips of paper which summarise the main idea in each part of the text. They then paperclip these labels to the margin at the appropriate place.

If photocopies cannot be made, and it is not possible physically to mark the passage in the book, you may have access to acetate sheets that can be laid over the page. Pupils can do the underlining on these sheets using wipe-off pens. However, the exercise of writing labels on slips of paper is always a feasible alternative and has the advantage of being useful for a variety of other purposes. For instance, the labels can be muddled up and re-organised in sequence by the pupils after the passage has been removed. Pupils can be invited to talk their way through the labels, reconstructing the meaning and thereby having an opportunity for making the new information their own. The labels can be used as the basis for a homework exercise, providing opportunities for writing about the topic without reference to the text book. They can also provide pupils with helpful reference material when they want to revise a topic.

For the pupils, this directed 'read' provides a structure for active engagement with the text and this is more likely to ensure that the pupils process the information on which you want them to focus. It enables pupils to 'pin down' those parts of the passage which are relevant to the task you have set for them. Also, this technique gives pupils practice in making judgements about passages – which aspects are important and which aspects can be ignored. It allows them to ask the questions: which details are relevant? what is this passage about? Different kinds of text, a descriptive history text or a mathematical part of a science text for instance, will be read very differently

using this sort of strategy. The significant points are likely to come at a much higher rate in the second text. The activity brings this to the attention of the pupils and encourages them to adjust their ways of reading to suit the demands of the two texts.

This last point, that different subject texts tend to call for different approaches to reading, has a crucial implication. This is that subject teachers must not abdicate their responsibility to help pupils read the texts *of their subject*. If, for example, special needs and English staff only help pupils to read novels they may become proficient at that sort of reading but still be poor at reading maths or French books. That is one reason why the DARTs activities discussed here, and in the following sections, should be part of the toolkit of all teachers. Another is that a subject teacher can actually do the DARTs activities themselves. This can reveal weaknesses in the content or structure of a text that may have gone unnoticed because that text had become very familiar to the teacher. Even if you do not go on to use DARTs activities with your pupils, and we would, of course, hope that you do, you will be in a better position to help pupils cope with these weaknesses.

b) Text completion

This activity is called 'text completion' because it requires pupils to reconstruct or complete the meaning of a passage from which certain parts have been deleted by the teacher.

Activity 6.3b

1. Having decided on a suitable passage for the lesson, delete words or phrases at those points where you want the pupils to think.

2. The choice of words or phrases to be deleted should be directly related to the teaching or learning outcomes which you require.

3. The choice of words or phrases is therefore quite deliberate and the pattern of deletions will be irregular, unlike the cloze procedure which is based on regular deletions.

The words or phrases which you choose to delete from the text for Activity 6.3b may be focused on the content of the passage or on the language of the written text. Choices may vary from subject to subject e.g.:

- In Science the focus is usually on the content of the text in terms of the scientific ideas or applications which it is putting forward.
- In English there may be a greater emphasis on the language used in the text. Here you might, for example, delete all the adjectives to encourage pupils to think about appropriate replacements and to argue about the appropriateness, vividness, power etc. of ideas put forward in the group.

The number of deletions will also vary, this time according to:

- the difficulty of the content of the text, and
- the background knowledge of the pupils.

Deletions in text which are of one word length are particularly useful in the area of language development. The reader can be forced to use syntactic and/or semantic cues in order to begin the process of finding the appropriate word to complete the text. Also it may be necessary for the reader to use ideas from earlier or later in the text (both forward and backward acting cues) thus highlighting a strategy which is often used by proficient readers: namely the use of the whole context of a piece of text to help to unravel its meaning.

Generally, *all* references to a particular idea in a text should *not* be deleted. If this is done, the reader is more likely to rely on guesswork to reconstruct the text, and may indeed be forced to do so by the lack of clues available. For example, consider the sentence, 'An infra-red camera forms an image from the different amounts of heat emitted from the warmer and cooler parts of the object.' This might be an early part of a text which is used with pupils to help them understand how such cameras work. If the words 'heat', 'warmer' and 'cooler' are all omitted in preparing the text for a text completion exercise, readers who knew nothing about infra-red cameras before coming to the text would be forced to guess what the words had been, and that will not help to improve their ability to understand text of this type. If one of these words is left in (and certainly if two are allowed to remain) the readers can work out what the omitted words were from the context, and that will be a reading skill that they can apply elsewhere. It will also, by making them think about what the text is saying, help them to remember this particular fact about infra-red cameras.

It will be clear from what has been said above that *careful preparation* of text completion exercises is required. We have already given some ideas for the choice of deletions. The presentation of the prepared passage is also important. The gaps which you make in the text should be of uniform length and you should provide a line to signify that text has been deleted. Don't forget to 'cue' the reader with a lead-in paragraph which has no deletions. In English, for example, an appreciation of the writer's style and vocabulary will be helped by this kind of 'lead-in', before reaching the first deletion.

c) Sequencing

This technique is another way of modifying a passage in order to promote 'a willingness and ability to reflect on what is being read'. It is used most effectively with passages of text which deal, for instance, with the steps in an experiment, or the phases in a process, or the stages in the development of a plot. It can also be used with worksheets giving instructions on how to do something, and can be useful in avoiding the sorts of problem which can arise if pupils start work without having read the whole sheet of instructions. It is important to remember that any passage treated as a sequencing exercise *must* have a sequential element as the pupil is presented with randomly ordered segments of the text and the purpose of the activity is to put them back into the right order. Descriptive texts of a country or of parts of a flower, for example, can really be written in any order so the sequencing activity is inappropriate with such material.

In Activity 6.3c pupils, either working in pairs or small groups, are required to re-order the text through discussion. They will be forced into using a 'broken' read as the passage itself is presented to them in a segmented fashion. Pupils will need to consider each section *and* the re-organisation of the whole passage to complete the activity. Importantly, this activity requires

Activity 6.3c

1. This activity consists of presenting pupils with a 'scrambled text' which has to be re-ordered to make sense.

2. The passage is 'scrambled' by printing sections of the passage on separate pieces of paper or card.

3. Each piece of paper or card should be the same size regardless of the amount of print which forms the particular section you have chosen.

4. Avoid the possibility of pupils disregarding the text and using, instead, physical aspects of the material to complete the sequence, e.g. matching edges of paper, fade lines etc.

5. If sections of text are mounted on durable card, the material can be used a number of times.

pupils to use sequential logic. It promotes discussion about clues within the passage, especially linguistic clues relating to time, e.g. 'After that', 'Lastly', 'It follows', 'Before', etc. The activity can therefore be used to illustrate the ways in which authors develop their ideas at the level of paragraphs.

The ordered passage can form part of the pupils' notes by being stuck or stapled into their notebooks or files for future reference.

d) Prediction

Group prediction exercises are helpful for the development of attentive reading as the pupils must use information from the whole text to inform their hypotheses about what may happen next.

Activity 6.3d

1. Choose material which has a clear line of development which can be either read aloud by you, or read by the pupils.

2. Break up the passage into sections which each contain enough information for speculation concerning what might follow.

3. Pupils are given instalments of the passage, in sequence, and they predict what follows.

4. These predictions take place in the first instance in small groups or pairs – coming together for class discussion later.

5. You will find it necessary to finish each instalment of the sectioned text with one or two questions to prompt the pupils' discussion.

Activity 6.3d requires pupils to justify their claims in the light of knowledge which they may already possess or information in the passage already read, or by using inferences based on the passage at each stage. Its purpose is to generate discussion and illustrate that what is contained in the text is a legitimate source of evidence for thought. During discussion pupils learn to modify their hypotheses and also learn how to marshall evidence to convince others of the validity of their point of view.

Reading part of a text and stopping at an exciting moment can also act as a strong motivation for pupils who do not read frequently of their own volition. This kind of 'tempting' activity is obviously valuable within the context of English, although it may also be suitable in other curriculum areas. For instance, the pupils could be asked to find out the last step in a process for homework.

e) Diagram and table completion

Activity 6.3e invites pupils to complete missing sections of tables or diagrams which relate to their reading of a passage. It is best preceded by the underlining and labelling activities (Section 6.3a) as these items of information will usually provide the key to solve the problem of missing information in the table or diagram.

See Section 6.3a, page 36.

Activity 6.3e

1. Choose a passage which has an accompanying diagram or table.

2. Mask out some or all of the information in the table or diagram, maybe information in the body of the table, maybe a row or a column heading.

3. How much you choose to mask out will depend upon whether the activity is used with new material or for revision purposes.

Having completed the underlining or labelling activity (Section 6.3a), pupils are now required to use that information in completing the diagram or table. Working in pairs or small groups, they are able to discuss their ideas together before finalising their decisions. The class discussion which follows enables each group to take part by contributing their solution to the problem.

The completed table or diagram can then be filed by each pupil and used as the basis for writing. This writing will then take place away from the original text, and will forestall the usual activity of copying directly from the text.

Some texts which describe a number of related events, for instance the changes in vegetation, bird and animal life as one goes up a mountain, lend themselves to tabular representation, although none may appear in the original text. The tables constructed from these texts provide pupils with useful revision material.

Useful further information can be found in Graham and Robinson (1984).

f) Consolidation of learning through oral work and writing

To ensure that pupils retain what they learn from reading they need opportunities for oral work and for writing. The aims of these two activities are not the same.

Oral discussion

1. Talk helps to clarify ideas.
2. Talk helps to share ideas.
3. Talk helps the pupils to make the language of the subject their own language.

Writing

1. Involves thinking through and clarifying ideas. (Copying from a text does not.)
2. Helps to focus attention on the vocabulary of the subject.
3. Consolidates the discussion and makes the knowledge the pupil's own.
4. Provides a permanent record of achievement for later reference.

When you ask pupils to learn from text, make opportunities for both of these necessary follow-up activities. It is the talking which helps pupils to forge the links between their own past experience and the new information presented in their reading. Writing will consolidate and capture this new learning for later reference.

g) Summary to Section 6.3

It is not envisaged that every text-based lesson will require the full range of strategies discussed in this section. However, they are examples of ways in which pupils can explore texts, using activities in small groups which they find fun and absorbing. As mentioned before, pupils with limited reading ability can join groups of able readers and take part in the meaning-making activity just as readily through the discussion and argument which is fostered. Indeed, their reading skills are often enhanced in this way.

An important aspect of activities which direct pupils reading activity and focus their attention on text is that they provide opportunities for group work and talk which is specific to the topic in hand. A further direct outcome of the activities is that you get a much clearer insight into the pupils' thinking and you can take the opportunity to evaluate the success of your teaching at each point. Remember these are *not* just activities for the English teacher. You can put them to use to encourage learning of *any* piece of content, in *any* subject. They are simply ways of getting pupils to use any written material in a more effective and absorbing way.

Because of the structure of these tasks and the accompanying discussion which will take place, these activities are useful for *all* pupils, including those with significant learning difficulties.

Activity 6.3g

- Try these ideas and see how they work for you.

- Prepare at least one lesson using these ideas for each group you will be teaching.

Further ideas of particular relevance to science teaching are given by Davies and Greene (1984), and more general advice can be found in Morris and Stewart-Dore (1984).

6.4 Teaching reading

a) Introduction

There may well be some pupils in the classes that you teach who have little or no reading ability. They will almost certainly be receiving support from the special needs staff, but it would be wise to check this out for yourself. You will need to know from these specialist teachers how to help such a pupil in your own class, so contact with them will be valuable. If you wish to get involved with teaching pupils to read under the supervision of the special needs staff, make sure that you follow their programme and reinforce what they are doing with that pupil.

Helpful references include:
  Kohl, H. (1974), *Reading, How to,* Penguin.
  Longley, C. (1977), *Reading After Ten,* BBC (see pages 46–9).
  Meek, M. (1983), *Achieving Literacy,* Routledge and Kegan Paul.
  Walker, C. (1974), *Reading Development and Extension,* Ward Lock
    (especially pages 102–104).

b) Slow readers

Slow readers, in contrast to slow learners, are pupils who simply read at a slow pace. This can be quite a disability both in and out of school. There are a variety of reasons for this disability, including many out-of-school factors, but much of the problem *can* be alleviated in school. The following paragraphs give some ideas on how this might be achieved. The information here is short, not because there is little to say on the subject, but because, as a mainstream teacher you will be offering this kind of help with reading under the guidance of a specialist teacher, and should ensure that your approach is consistent with his or her way of working with the pupils.

Some pupils in secondary schools are still at the stage where they have to read each word, either out loud or sub-vocally, and this means that their reading cannot progress faster than the speed of speech. In order to overcome this, these pupils require reading material which is much easier than their peers, and they need to be encouraged to read for pure pleasure. Emphasis on your part needs to be less on the accuracy of the pupils' reading and more on whether they understand the content of what they have been reading.

The most easily observable slow reader is one who reads word-by-word, an activity which is usually accompanied by finger-pointing. One way of overcoming this difficulty is to provide the pupils with a reading 'window'. This is a piece of card the size of a page in the pupil's book which has a line-sized slot one quarter way down the card. The pupil treats this slot as a viewing window and reads each line by moving the card down the page. Gradually increase the window to two and then three lines depth. Beyond this, the pupil will not need the card any longer. To ensure that pupils do not return to word by word reading and finger-pointing, encourage them to use both hands to hold the book.

When working with individual pupils and hearing them read aloud, there are a number of things which can help slow readers. Some are mentioned in Activity 6.4b.

44

Activity 6.4b

1. You can take it in turns to read some of the text with the pupil, for instance, line by line, or page by page.

2. Set the pupil a purpose to the reading and encourage the pupil to skim and scan the text for information.

3. Ask the pupil to read a paragraph silently, and then aloud to you.

4. Ask the pupil questions about the reading without having to read aloud to you.

5. The pupil tape-records his/her own reading aloud, and listens to the recording following the text on his/her own.

Make sure that the sessions which you share with a pupil are relaxed and enjoyed by you both. After the session the pupil could be sent away with a specific piece of information to locate, which would encourage quick scanning of a whole paragraph rather than word by word reading. As a reader, the pupil needs to develop a growing awareness of the function of reading, rather than just the techniques of the activity.

Clearly, such an approach places a great emphasis on the content of reading rather than the accuracy of the task. Useful sources of further information are Arnold (1982) and Longley (1977).

c) Using printed material

Some pupils have not been shown how to locate information in text books and reference books and many of them have not worked out how to do this for themselves. It is worth spending a little time making sure that your pupils can make the most of their opportunities for independent study.

Do this by drawing their attention to aspects of books which are additional to the continuous prose: e.g. tables of contents, section headings, the index, the glossary, the bibliography. Develop their skill in using these devices by activities such as Activity 6.4c.

Activity 6.4c

1. Ask the pupils to find the contents list of a book and help them to do so if they have difficulty.

2. Explain that this is where they can find a list of chapter titles and section headings which will give clues as to what each chapter or section is about.

3. Ask them questions which focus their attention on a search procedure. Ask, for instance, 'Which chapter should I read to find out about X? Which section or sub-section will help me most?'

Use similar techniques to help pupils use the other sources of this kind of information in a book (the index etc).

Help pupils to use more general sources of information (dictionaries, encyclopaedias, library catalogues) in a similar way.

Frequently we direct pupils' attention to page numbers of books for homework or for a class activity. Remember that it will be more helpful on some occasions to leave the searching procedure to the pupils after providing guidance and practice of the kind outlined above.

6.5 Readability of printed material

a) Introduction

Which factors in the context of reading can provide difficulty for the reader? There are many, some of which are listed below:

1. In the *reader:*   motivation, interest, background and familiarity with the content and vocabulary.

2. In the *print:*   type size, leading, format and lay-out.

3. In the *content:*   fact, fiction, topic or information.

4. In the *language:*   vocabulary, grammar, complexity of structures, style.

In measuring the difficulty of a particular book or passage, it is usually those features which can be counted which are significant. These features tend to be focused on the linguistic properties of the text. Features which have been reckoned to contribute towards the difficulty of a text are the *words* – their length and rarity; the *sentences* – their length and degree of complexity; the *ideas* and *concepts*; the *references* and *allusions* to experience in common between the writer and the reader. One way of measuring text difficulty is to use readability formulae.

b) Readability formulae

There is a variety of what are referred to as 'readability formulae' which make use of word and/or sentence length in selected passages in order to establish the difficulty level of a book or passage (Gulliland, 1972; Harrison, 1980). An example of one of the simplest formulae is given in Activity 6.5b.

Activity 6.5b

Smog grading for readability
1. Count ten consecutive sentences near the beginning, middle and end of the book or passage.

2. In these thirty sentences, count all the words which have three or more syllables.

3. Estimate the square root of the number of polysyllabic words counted in this way.

4. Add eight to this approximate square root – this will give the age of the pupils for which the book or passage is appropriate.

Use of formulae

The application of different readability formulae can be very time consuming and they require the systematic selection of samples of text varying in number and length. It must also be remembered that the formulae may mislead because not all long words are difficult to read, and because sentence construction and content determine the difficulty of a passage, not necessarily sentence length.

Results obtained from the use of readability formulae therefore need to be treated cautiously. Their accuracy is limited to a range of three years, which means that when a readability formula result indicates the reading level of a text book as appropriate for thirteen year olds, all that can be relied upon is that the text is likely to be suitable for twelve or fourteen year olds as well – not very helpful information for the busy teacher. What the results of these formulae *will* enable you to do is to identify gross mismatches between books and their intended readers, and to rank your text books in order of difficulty so that, if a pupil has difficulty with one, you have a firm basis for choosing another with which s/he is more likely to succeed.

c) Writing for pupils

Clearly there are other aspects of difficulty in text which are not measured by formulae (Perera, 1980, 1986). These, together with the results of formulae should be borne in mind when assessing the difficulty of a book. They are also useful in reminding you of pitfalls to avoid in your own writing for pupils, e.g. in worksheet design etc.

Activity 6.5c
Guard against creating unnecessary difficulties in your own writing for pupils. Be aware of any difficult passages in text books that you use with pupils and plan how you will help the pupils to overcome the difficulty.

One area in which you should be particularly careful to guard against linguistic difficulty is in writing your own worksheets for pupils. We therefore finish this chapter with some brief advice on this issue.

Making your own worksheets

Some points to take into consideration are given in the following list:

1. Lines of type should be about four inches long (about 10 words per line).
2. Words in lower case are easier to read than words in capitals.
3. Italic print is the most difficult to read. Use italics only when emphasis is required.
4. The size of typeface is important but depends on many factors (line length, inter-word spacing, inter-line spacing). A standard typewriter face with double spacing is usually adequate. It is the space between the lines which is more important than the size of the print.
5. The maximum number of vowels on an A4 sheet should not exceed 480. The number of words *in this section* is 388, and there are over 700 vowels!
6. Use active sentences, they are easier to understand then passive ones.
   cf. 'Safety belts must always be worn'
   'Always wear your safety belt'
   or 'Clunk, Click every trip'.

7. Improve the interest of the passage by the use of 'personal words' and 'personal sentences'.

Personal words are:
   a) All 1st, 2nd and 3rd person pronouns except the neuter pronouns.
   b) All words that have masculine or feminine natural gender (Jones, May, father, milkman etc.)
      Group words (people etc.)

Personal sentences are:
   a) Spoken sentences marked by quotation marks.
   b) Questions, commands, requests etc. directly addressed to the reader.
   c) Exclamations.

8. Positive statements are easier to understand than negative statements.

   'Do you disagree with the statement that 7 is not a negative number?'

9. A summary before the instructions can help a reader to organise his or her learning.

10. Headings and sub-headings can help the reader to organise his or her reading.

11. Headings in the form of questions are particularly effective.

12. Simple line drawings are often more effective than more complex drawings, or even photographs. The simple line drawing can concentrate on the salient points.

13. Bar charts are easier to read than tables of results.

14. Pupils prefer the text in a worksheet to be typed, but they prefer diagram labels to be handwritten.

15. Avoid the superfluous … 'Having examined this topic thoroughly we are now in a position to …'

16. Check for continuity: change of subject, change of tense.

17. Ensure that the main 'message' on a page is given sufficient prominence. Do not add extra material to avoid blank spaces.

18. Avoid long sentences. The average sentence length is about 20 words but the immediate memory span is only 7 words.

Published worksheet material for pupils is also vulnerable to these sources of difficulty. Check them thoroughly before expecting pupils to work from them. You may find it necessary to support the material with oral work on your part. Remember that having pupils work collaboratively often helps them to overcome some of the difficulties which printed materials can present.

Writing

7

7.1 Introduction

There are several different reasons for asking pupils to write something. For example, they can be asked to write in order to make a record for future use by them or by others. On other occasions, the purpose can be to help pupils to clarify and consolidate understanding through the writing process in which pupils organise their thoughts and translate subject language into their own words.

Because of this variety of purposes, it is important to make sure that pupils are clear about the topic and context for any writing which you want them to undertake and, especially, to ensure that they understand the purpose and the audience for the writing before the activity begins. The writing which you require from pupils may be individual, personal or private, or it may be group negotiated and written by more than one contributor. Whatever the method of writing adopted, do not always pressure pupils to complete an acceptable finished piece at one sitting.

It is always helpful if pupils become involved in talking before writing takes place. This talk among themselves or with you will give support and direction to their writing. It enables group consideration of possibilities, of leads forward, and of the shaping and clarifying of ideas. Perhaps, during this first stage it will become apparent that they need to do more research through reading or delving into other resources.

7.2 Organising writing activities

1. Writing can often, with value, be preceded by a period in which pupils discuss the content and nature of the task they are being asked to do.

2. Asking pupils to write is not the only way of providing them with a record of the lesson. Ask yourself whether other options may sometimes lead to more useful records, as well as being a more efficient use of pupils' time.

3. Writing should be addressed to many audiences, not only to you. Pupils should know who they are writing for. Wherever possible the product of their work should be made available to the intended audience. That is, if you ask them to write something 'for next year's first year' it should be used by next year's first year. Where possible there should be some feedback, even if only

50

of a general kind, from that audience. These things make writing appear to be what it is: namely a useful way of communicating ideas, not just an exercise for the teacher to mark.

4. Writing can be improved by sharing ideas with a writing group. For example, other pupils engaged on a similar task should exchange drafts and discuss them.

5. Writing can be used to encourage learning. It is not just a means of assessing pupils.

6. Writing can be prompted by reading. You can organise the task to ensure that this does not simply lead to pupils copying out chunks of texts.

7. Writing should be used as a reading resource by other pupils.

8. Can you think of any more.........?

7.3 Content in written work

A procedure which can encourage all pupils to produce good written work and which can be supportive of those who have particular difficulties is set out below. Use all or part of the procedure in connection with some of the writing tasks you set for pupils. It is important to acknowledge to your pupils that writing is difficult; the stages involved include thinking about what to write and how it is to be organised, choosing appropriate language and then getting spelling and handwriting acceptable. It is just not possible to get all this right at one sitting. Make sure that your pupils are aware of these steps and stages. Let them know which part of the overall activity of writing should be the focus of their attention at any one time.

a) Rough drafts

The purpose of a rough draft is to record ideas for later review. This activity will involve a lot of talking, and it may well produce messy writing with lots of additions, deletions, arrows indicating the re-positioning of words and/or phrases, words misspelled, punctuation missing and sentences imperfectly formed. These faults do not matter at this stage as this first draft is an attempt to get ideas down on paper, to select and organise information, and to try out ways of articulating thoughts.

b) Writing conference

The conference takes place between a pupil and teacher during drafting, and may help some pupils to clarify ideas and talk through ways of expressing them. This activity requires the kind of classroom organisation which enables you to move freely, systematically, and interestedly among the pupils. It implies intervention in the writing process on your part not as the marker of the finished product, but rather allowing pupils to use you in a consultative capacity – enabling you to seek information from them as opposed to the other way round.

c) Reading to review writing

Once rough copies have been drafted, these can be exchanged within informal groups for pupils to read each other's work. They can be encouraged to discuss content, arrangement of ideas, expression and surface techniques among themselves. The object of this reading activity is to improve on individual pieces of writing, by clarifying what was intended to be conveyed to a reader, expanding on incomplete ideas and suggesting where changes can be made. This review stage can be done individually, but you know from your own writing experiences that what is clear to you may not be clear to another reader, so group work will be important at this stage.

d) Re-drafting

Re-drafting of rough drafts and discussion notes may be lengthy and will involve:

1. Re-thinking ideas on the basis of relevant comments.
2. Re-shaping ideas to express them more precisely.
3. The re-ordering, editing out or addition of new information.

e) Editing

When pupils have reworked their ideas and forms of expression into a whole piece of writing, they will be ready to start editing. This process takes the 'wrinkles' out of the writing by attending to the surface features of spelling, punctuation and grammar. Once again you should use this editing stage as an opportunity to help individual pupils with any difficulties which they may be experiencing. For instance, encouraging them to use a dictionary or thesaurus. Make sure you take a dictionary to all lessons, so that pupils can borrow it for reference.

f) Final copy

The final copy is prepared by the pupil for sharing with others, either for display and/or assessment. The audience for whom the writing was created is now given a chance to read it and to respond. This response may take several forms either orally or in writing. Remember that our response to pupils' writing needs to combine both sensitivity and genuine interest. A tick, combined with a mark out of ten is never appropriate, but a written response to the *content* is an indicator that the piece has been read and understood and this can serve as a powerful motivator.

Caution
Too frequently, the process of re-writing has been used as a punitive measure by teachers. Pupils regard the request to re-write as an indication that they have 'got it wrong'.

Therefore, the procedure outlined above may not be popular.

You will have to think how you introduce the procedure to pupils.

You may find it best to demonstrate to them the necessity for this procedure with a piece of your own writing.

More useful ideas about the teaching of writing can be found in Thornton (1980) and in Spencer (1983). As in the case of reading, it is important that all teachers help pupils with their writing through the medium of their subject. Styles and expectations, audiences and kinds of use for writing all differ from subject to subject. Pupils whose attention is drawn explicitly to writing in just one subject (perhaps English) will inevitably have a narrow view of what it is about, and how to set about writing for themselves.

7.4 Handwriting

a) Introduction

Research has shown that when they mark pupils' work, from class books or examination papers, teachers' judgements are influenced by the pupils' handwriting. This can lead to erroneous decisions concerning, for instance, the ability of a pupil and the marks which are given for a piece of work. In some cases poor handwriting may be used by a pupil to mask uncertain spelling. Another reason could be related to the fact that the pupil lacks confidence in what they have written and their poor handwriting ensures that no one will be able to read it. For whatever reason, because of the positive influence of good handwriting, you need to help pupils to develop a conventionally acceptable style.

The Bullock Report (1975) adds further that … 'the ability to write easily, quickly and legibly affects the quality of children's written output, for difficulty with handwriting can hamper the flow of thoughts and limit fluency.' (Section 11.51)

b) Reasons for poor handwriting

1. Clumsiness, sometimes viewed as carelessness.
2. Inappropriate letter formation.
3. A tightly gripped pen, or the arm and hand tense, can result in jagged writing.
4. Racing to get down notes, struggling to copy accurately, and experiencing difficulties with spelling all interfere with the flow of writing. The result is that overall presentation becomes irrelevant.
5. Writing that is too small is often an effort to cover mistakes, or a sign of uncertainty about the work.

Activity 7.4b

1. Examine *your own* handwriting.

2. Now that you are a teacher, your writing in pupils' books and on the blackboard will provide them with an important model.

3. Is you handwriting suitable for this purpose? Is it clear?

c) How to help

1. If you suspect that letters are inappropriately formed, watch the pupil(s) writing to see exactly how they form their letters. You will then be better able to help them. For example, it may help the pupil who tackles each letter in a different way to know that letters do share formation patterns.

a, o, g, d, qu, c

For instance: all these involve an anti-clockwise circle or part circle.

m, n, h, r, t, l

all involve a vertical downstroke; the first four involve a 'bounce' at the bottom of that downstroke.

2. Pupils with handwriting difficulties find it helpful to write on lined paper or to use writing guidelines under their piece of paper.

3. Many pupils need help in joining letters together. Show them how to join an 'easy' letter with every letter of the alphabet (for instance, *1a*, *1b*, *1c*, etc). Also show them how to do this with more difficult combinations such as ba, *bb*, *bc* etc.

4. Watch the way in which pupils position their page while they write. Left handers will need to slant the page in the opposite direction to right handers in order to reveal what they are writing as they write. Also the page should be placed on the appropriate (left) side of the midline of the body.

5. Plastic triangular pencil 'sleeves' help pupils to correct a faulty grip and also help to position the grip appropriately.

Finally, when concentrating on handwriting, define with the pupils the *target* for each session. This might be spacing, letter formation, crossing out technique, organisation etc. *Monitor* the pupils' performance so that they can see their own progress. Remember that 'nothing succeeds like success'.

More details on helping pupils with handwriting problems can be found in Sassoon (1983) and in Gordon and McKinlay (1980).

d) Copying from the blackboard or other material

Many teachers regard 'copying from the board' as an unproblematic part of lessons for pupils, which makes few demands on their ability. For some pupils it is, however, a difficult task and the errors they make are not necessarily a sign of laziness or lack of care.

Although pupils may be able to read a word on the board, they may not be able to remember it for long enough to copy it down accurately. When copying, they look back to their own book and cannot remember how to spell the word, they look up again and find the place, although it may be the wrong place, and then they look back to their book. While copying a long word they may have to look up and down several times, generating the possibility of inaccuracy on each occasion. These memory problems (see Figure 3.1 on page 12) are accompanied by other difficulties. For example the pupils have to transform what is presented on the board in a vertical plane, into writing in their books in a horizontal plane. Also, they have to continually change the focus of their eyes from the long range required to read the board to the short range required to read their own writing. Some pupils find this tiring and difficult.

When the class is asked to copy from the blackboard, you can give pupils with this difficulty two alternative activities. They can 'read' the text into a tape recorder and then take it down later in their own time, or they can be given ready-prepared notes, either to stick into their books or to copy from.

If the text to be copied is on such a set of notes, or if it is in a book, pupils can be asked to place a card or marker under the line they are copying. This will substantially reduce the time taken and the number of errors. This makes copying from a book easier than copying from a blackboard. Copying from a book is also easier because the text to be copied is horizontal. The problem of optical accommodation is also very much reduced, because the distance between the eye and the book, and the eye and their own page of notes is the same.

Activity 7.4d
Make sure that you know which pupils in your class should be wearing glasses, and that they do. Also make sure that they do not sit at the back of the class as this may make blackboard work even more difficult for them.

e) Letter confusions

The letters 'b' and 'd' are difficult for some children who have not formed stable left-right concepts. Activity 7.4e explains an easy way to correct this.

Activity 7.4e

1. Ask the pupil to pick up a felt-tipped pen in the hand usually used for writing.

2. If the pupils are right-handed ask them to hold the other hand up palm facing, like this:

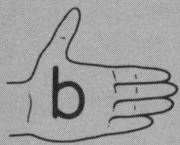

3. With the felt-tipped pen get them to draw a 'b' – ascender down the thumb, extension round the palm.

4. In a page or two of print point to some 'b's and ask the pupil, 'What is that?' Make sure that the hand is held up and the letter is checked. After the looking and checking and correct identification is made 10 to 20 times, point to a 'd'. Get the pupil to check their answer. Say, 'Yes' that is not the "b". Remember you always know the "b" because you can pick up a pen and write it on yourself.'

5. A left-hander, of course, is only taught that they have a 'd' to write on their hand. (Ask them to keep it written on the hand for the rest of the day – and write it again next day if it helps. Often just holding up the hand is necessary to remind the pupil.)

6. NB **You only teach one letter.**

7. If the difficulty is between 'p' and 'q' use the back of the hand, and then the thumb becomes the descender.

Remember that young children just learning to read and write frequently confuse letters but they develop techniques of *self-correction,* and are encouraged to do so by primary teachers.

The above technique is suitable for those children in later primary or secondary stages who have been unable to establish self-correction on this specific problem.

7.5 Spelling

a) Introduction

The Bullock Report (DES, 1975), in its discussion of spelling, states that ... 'it is a convention that matters.' (Para 11.42) 'In the first place confidence in spelling frees children to write to fulfil their purpose. In the second place spelling disability is an undoubted social handicap in society.' (Para 11.43).

It used to be thought that if children could read then they should be able to spell. Children who were good readers and poor spellers were considered to be lazy or too hurried in their work. Recent research has shed much light on this difficulty and we can now tackle it with confidence. Good spellers have been found to possess at least three of the following characteristics:

- good verbal intelligence;
- good visual perception;
- swift handwriting;
- they are careful;
- good self-image as regards spelling.

The last characteristic is probably the most important of all.

In order to foster good spelling you must be consistent in your approach with pupils. Also if you think good spelling is important and help your pupils to achieve it, you will have good spellers in your classes.

b) Suggestions for fostering good spelling

Activity 7.5b

1. Interest the pupils in words. For instance find root words within a word and get the pupils to see the connection between them. For example: 'musician' is easier to spell if you realise it links with 'music'.

2. Collect word families, e.g. 'ought', 'bought' etc.

3. Pay attention to letter clusters, e.g. 'ant, 'sion' etc.

4. Four or five words tested each day is a more effective teaching routine than twenty words tested once a week.

5. Have dictionaries available and show pupils how to use them.

6. Teach children a strategy for getting spelling right (see page 56).

c) Steps in learning to spell

An effective way of teaching pupils to learn to spell is as follows:

1. The pupil *prints* the word correctly on a small card, having checked the correct spelling with you or a dictionary.

2. The pupil uses the card and follows this procedure:

LOOK   The pupil looks at the word with the intention of remembering it. This involves going on looking at the word until they can see it with their eyes shut i.e. 'in their mind's eye'.

COVER   They cover the word by turning the card over.

WRITE   They *write* the word without stopping.

CHECK   They check their word with the one on the card.

3. The pupil repeats this procedure four or five times. They do not correct individual letters or syllables. Remember, they repeat the *complete* procedure on *whole* words. It usually takes two or three attempts to get a word correct using this method.

Then

4. On other days repeat Nos. **2** and **3** above as often as required until the pupil is sure that they know the word(s).

5. At this stage, get pupils to test each other. If they spell the word correctly during this activity they can put a tick on the back of the card.

6. On the next occasion, repeat Nos. **2, 3** and **5**. Pupils can tick cards for a second time if they have correctly spelled the word again.

7. Pupils should collect three ticks in this way. Don't forget to leave a period of time between each of these testing sessions.

8. Pupils should keep a list of words learned in this way to serve as a record of progress and of 'tricky' words. Alphabet ordered word books, or books in which words are grouped by curriculum areas in which they frequently appear can be valuable resources for individual pupils.

(Leah, 1982)

d) Good readers who are poor spellers

Pupils who are good readers can sometimes, unexpectedly, turn out to be poor spellers.

These unexpected poor spellers appear to use different strategies for reading and for writing. They have learned to read 'by eye' but they write 'by ear'. The good speller retains the visual image of the word, the poor speller relies on the sound of the word. The routine outlined above of LOOK, COVER, WRITE, CHECK will also help this group of pupils as it is a strategy for reinforcing the visual imagery of words and for building up the visual memory.

e) Do's and don'ts in teaching spelling

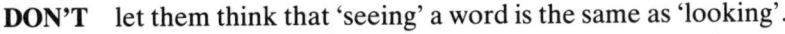

DO make sure that children always write from memory. If they copy, they often adopt a letter by letter strategy which does not help them to get the whole word into the tips of their fingers.

DO help pupils with their handwriting. A fast flowing hand helps to reinforce accurate motor responses.

DO encourage them to be careful.

DO give lots of praise for all their efforts.

DON'T let them think that 'seeing' a word is the same as 'looking'.

DON'T ever let them copy.

DON'T let them sound out words they want to spell.

DON'T get worried by every little slip.

DON'T let them think that they are poor spellers.

(Cripps, 1983)

When marking written work, resist the temptation to correct every spelling mistake. Choose three or four words which the pupil frequently misspells and present these for the procedure outlined in Section (c) above. It may be appropriate, on some occasions, to mark all the words a pupil has *correctly* spelled. Remember the importance of retaining the pupil's good self-image with respect to their spelling ability and how powerful this can be in helping them to become confident and successful spellers.

Further advice on helping pupils with spelling difficulties can be found in Peters (1985).

8

Communicating with specialist teachers

8.1 Introduction

In Chapter 1 of this book, we argued that a full response to pupils with special needs in a school must involve all members of staff. The aim of Chapters 2 to 7 has been largely to provide some practical advice to help you turn this general exhortation into a reality. However we also mentioned in Chapter 1 that the special needs staff have an important role to play, in providing background information on pupils, giving further advice on techniques and materials for mainstream staff and, especially for pupils with complex or severe difficulties, making direct support available to the pupils themselves.

If this joint responsibility for special needs pupils is to be effectively discharged by mainstream and specialist staff, there must be good communication between them. The purpose of this short chapter is to suggest ways of making this communication effective.

As suggested above, the emphasis in this chapter is on communication between mainstream staff and special needs teachers. However, the mainstream teacher in a secondary school, particularly the student teacher, the probationer or the teacher new to the school, might also look to other colleagues for information and advice about dealing with pupils who have special needs. Form tutors and senior pastoral staff, the head of department in which the teacher works, senior staff in other departments (e.g. English and maths staff), or any senior teacher in charge of student teachers, in-service training and staff development, could all be valuable sources of information about pupils and advice on techniques and materials which the teacher might use. The points made on page 60 apply equally well to communication with staff of this kind.

8.2 What information do you need and how do you get it?

You need to know:

1. Background information about the pupil – particularly the pupil's general ability, specific strengths and weaknesses and the extent to which the pupil has difficulties in other subjects.

2. The support which other people (e.g. special needs staff) are providing for the pupil.

3. Techniques (like those in this book) that *you* could use to help the pupil in your lessons.

4. Special resources (equipment or written material) that are available in school that you could use to help the pupil.

Ask yourself who, in the structure of your school, is likely to know these things. Once the appropriate sources have been identified, information about the pupil and the support being provided elsewhere is largely factual and can be collected by making a simple request to the right person. However getting good advice about techniques or resources which you could profitably use with a given pupil is not so easy.

Activity 8.2
How to find out about techniques and resources:

First
1. Make specific observations of the pupil's difficulties. Use the checklists on pages 7–9 to guide you.
2. Try some of the activities mentioned in this book and keep a record of things that worked and things that did not.
3. Keep examples of the pupil's work.

Then

4. Talk to relevant staff in the school using the information that you have gathered in **1** to **3** above to give precision and structure to your discussion.

You cannot really expect to get good advice from a specialist teacher if all you can say about pupils is that they seem to have difficulties in your class. If you can describe those difficulties more fully, and especially if you can say that you have tried x and y and that x worked but y didn't, then the specialist has something to go on and is more likely to be able to give useful advice. The situation is closely analagous to calling an RAC patrol and saying 'My car won't start' or calling and saying 'The starter motor turns and the engine fires but it won't keep running.' In the second case you might well get some advice which will get you on your way.

The process discussed above is important, but it is not the whole story. When you have contacted a specialist teacher, or a form tutor or head of department, and have received advice on what to do you should try out the ideas *and report back on successes and failures to the staff concerned.* In this way they get feedback and can improve their own effectiveness as advisers, you get further advice if it is needed, and the pupil's situation is kept under review so that, if direct help from the specialist teacher seems necessary, it can be provided.

Finally, in some cases, advice will be needed from professionals outside school. There will be a system for contacting such professionals, probably through the special needs department, through senior pastoral staff or through the headteacher. You would be wise to find out about this system so that, should the need arise, you know how to make the necessary contacts. In another book in the series, *Organising the School's Response,* we discuss the roles on external professionals at greater length. This could be useful in raising your awareness of the range of people who might be of service to you or to the pupil with special needs, and of the characteristics of their different jobs.

Some general points

9.1 Getting it together

The previous chapters have provided advice about specific aspects of learning difficulty. It may be useful to carry out the general co-ordinating task given in Activity 9.1, in which these specific points, and other ideas which you have devised or drawn from other sources, can be drawn together.

Activity 9.1

1. Find out what the pupil already knows. (The checklists on pages 7 to 9 will help.) Beware of making assumptions about this.

2. Plan to start your teaching a little further back from where the pupil's understanding has reached – but not too far back.

Remember to plan your work in such a way that it builds on and consolidates what is already understood by the pupil.

3. Plan steps towards your teaching goal – smaller steps will be necessary when learning difficulties are more severe.

Incorporate the ideas from the rest of this book (e.g. selecting and using text, writing worksheets, developing thinking, supporting pupils with mathematical problems) in your plans.

4. Make specific generalisations both within and beyond the subject matter in hand to encourage meaningful rather than rote learning.

5. Take care to review pupils' progress, record how they respond to your initiatives, and be ready to adjust your plans in the light of their response.

6. Seek advice and support from other members of staff if the strategies you are using to help pupils are not being successful.

9.2 Slow learners in mixed ability classes

The points made throughout this book are, of course, just as applicable to the context of the mixed ability class as to any other. Indeed the more individualised nature of some mixed ability teaching provides an ideal setting in which to adjust material and teaching approaches for individual pupils in the ways which we have been suggesting. However, the problem of the pupil with learning difficulties in the mixed ability class has attracted much attention and there is a great deal of general advice available in the literature. Bell and Kerry (1982) mention ten points in particular.

1. Eliminate 'dead' time
Think about what you are going to do with pupils who finish work sooner than others. Have additional work ready for them or invite them to join slower groups.

2. Set a variety of tasks
Think of a range of different activities for the same teaching purpose. They should be designed to make use of the different skills and abilities of the pupils. Also, several small linked activities devoted to the same teaching point will be more successful than a single long activity.

3. Give instructions clearly
Never rely solely on written instructions. Make sure that you go over instructions with the pupils. Written instructions can be useful as a summary of what is to be done.

4. Revise any key points
Ask the pupils to reflect on, talk about and/or write about key points in the light of their own experience.

5. Sustain interest and motivation
Feed, but don't overwhelm, curiosity. Use competition sparingly, use cooperation and collaboration generously. Always give praise for pupils' efforts.

6. Encourage participation
Make sure that all pupils have a contribution to make to the lesson.

7. Give individual attention
Find as many times as possible to do this (e.g. when other pupils are occupied, breaks, lunchtimes, after school etc.).

8. Promote a confident classroom climate
Be consistent in your expectations of pupil behaviour and in your own responses to this.

9. Keep careful records
These will help you to identify difficulties early. Also they remind you of the progress which pupils are making.

10. Do not ignore the feedback from homework
If several pupils make errors in their homework this may reflect on your last lesson. Go over key points to sort out the difficulties.

This list of practical 'tips' can usefully be supplemented by some ideas from an interesting strand of research which is just becoming more widely known in teaching. This is the research area known as Aptitude-Treatment Interaction (ATI) research. It seeks to explore the possibility that pupils with different characteristics respond in different ways to different styles of teaching.

Some ATI results are quite interesting in relation to pupils with learning difficulties. Studies have shown that less able pupils responded better to small step, programmed learning using orderly sequences of ideas and continuous, overt feedback and correction than they did to conventional teaching. More able pupils, on the other hand, responded equally well to both styles. This is consistent with our description of pupils with learning difficulties in Chapter 3, where we argued that they had difficulty with planning a problem-solving strategy. The small-step style provides much more of the structure for the pupils to use.

Similarly, ATI studies showed that less able pupils achieved more when teaching was based on a deductive model, starting from a general point and deducing specific outcomes, whereas more able pupils achieved more when teaching was inductive, starting from a large number of examples and deriving a general rule. Other important findings are that less able pupils get more out of lessons which are structured mainly on the basis of their own previous or naive understanding of the topic (see Section 3.2e) whereas more able pupils are handicapped by this approach and achieve more when lessons are based on the logical content of the material.

Not all ATI studies used ability as the way of categorising pupils. It has been shown, for example, that highly anxious pupils were handicapped by open unstructured lesson styles which did not in any way handicap pupils who were more secure.

A feature of ATI research is that findings are rarely entirely conclusive, and replications of experiments sometimes lead to contradictory results. One should not, therefore, take the results quoted above, or other ATI results, as cast iron presciptions of what should or should not be done in the classroom. They do, however, provide valuable starting points for the teacher who wishes to develop his or her teaching by trying things out in a sensitive fashion, monitoring what goes on and modifying practice in the light of this monitoring. They alert enquiring, questioning teachers to variables which might profitably be taken into account in their attempts to improve their practice with particular groups of pupils.

Readers who wish to explore ATI research in detail should refer to Cronbach and Snow (1977) where the authors provide a detailed survey of ATI findings and a searching critique of the methodology and interpretation of ATI studies. This is far from an easy read, but it does offer a rich source of potentially useful ideas.

9.3 Models of teaching

This point about the importance of an enquiring style in seeking to develop one's practice in teaching leads us to summarise what we have offered in this book by presenting two models of teaching. Neither should be taken too literally, but they serve to remind you of the points we have made.

In the *first model* (Figure 9.3a), the response to a learning difficulty on the part of an individual pupil or group of pupils, is to *repeat the same piece of teaching using the same techniques and resources*. Notice that no direct assessment of the learning difficulty is made and that no additional background information is used.

If the piece of teaching did not work first time, in all probability it will not be much more effective next time. Therefore, this model is unlikely to be successful.

Figure 9.3a

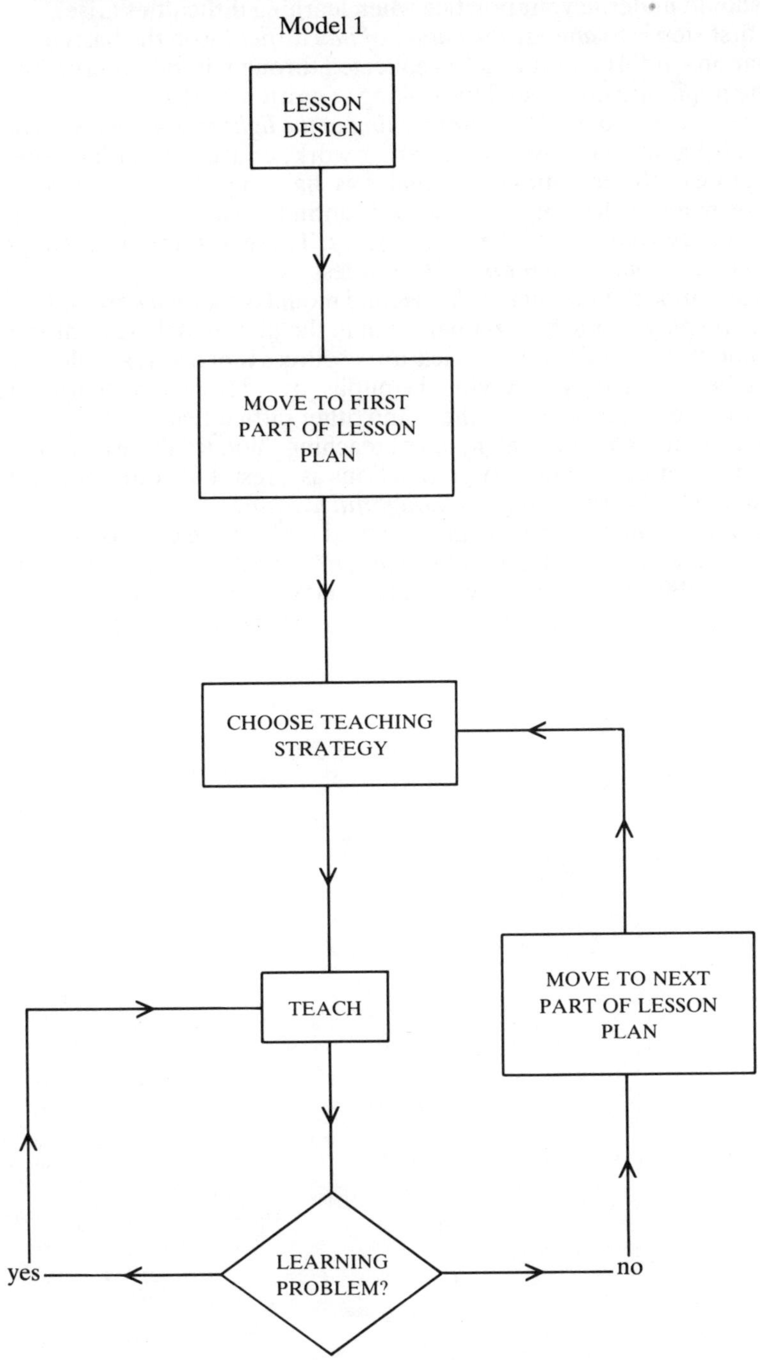

Model 1

```
            ┌──────────────┐
            │   LESSON     │
            │   DESIGN     │
            └──────┬───────┘
                   │
                   ▼
            ┌──────────────┐
            │ MOVE TO FIRST│
            │ PART OF LESSON│
            │    PLAN      │
            └──────┬───────┘
                   │
                   ▼
        ┌──────────────────┐
        │ CHOOSE TEACHING  │◄──────────┐
        │    STRATEGY      │           │
        └────────┬─────────┘           │
                 │                      │
                 ▼               ┌──────────────┐
        ┌──────────┐             │ MOVE TO NEXT │
  ┌────►│  TEACH   │             │ PART OF LESSON│
  │     └────┬─────┘             │    PLAN      │
  │          │                   └──────▲───────┘
  │          ▼                          │
  │      ╱────────╲                     │
 yes ◄──╱ LEARNING ╲──► no ─────────────┘
        ╲ PROBLEM? ╱
         ╲────────╱
```

The *second model* (Figure 9.3b) of teaching involves the kind of procedure which should underlie your practice when learning difficulties arise.

The first step is to *analyse the nature of that difficulty* on the basis of information – information which is collected through literal observation of what the pupils are doing, and by looking at written work etc.

The next step is to *modify your teaching in the light of your assessment*. This may involve going back over some earlier work, or using different visual aids, or using one of the activities or strategies we have suggested in this book.

Having made such changes you would continue to assess the effect and to further modify your approaches if necessary. There is, therefore, always an element of *continuous monitoring* in your lessons.

Another important aspect of this second model is that *background information* plays a much larger part than in the first model. This information will be about the pupils and the back-up resources that are available to you. This will be collected by observing the pupils, by reference to records and by talking to other teachers about these and other difficulties.

Model 2 is an experimental model of teaching. You try things out, you observe their effect and modify your actions as a result of your observations. It is first and foremost a *model of thoughtful teaching*.

Sometimes Model 2 can be applied in 'real time' in the classroom. Sometimes the assessment and subsequent modification of your teaching will take place between one lesson with a class and the next. In either situation, it is a model which will help you to be more responsive to your pupils' needs.

Figure 9.3b   Model 2

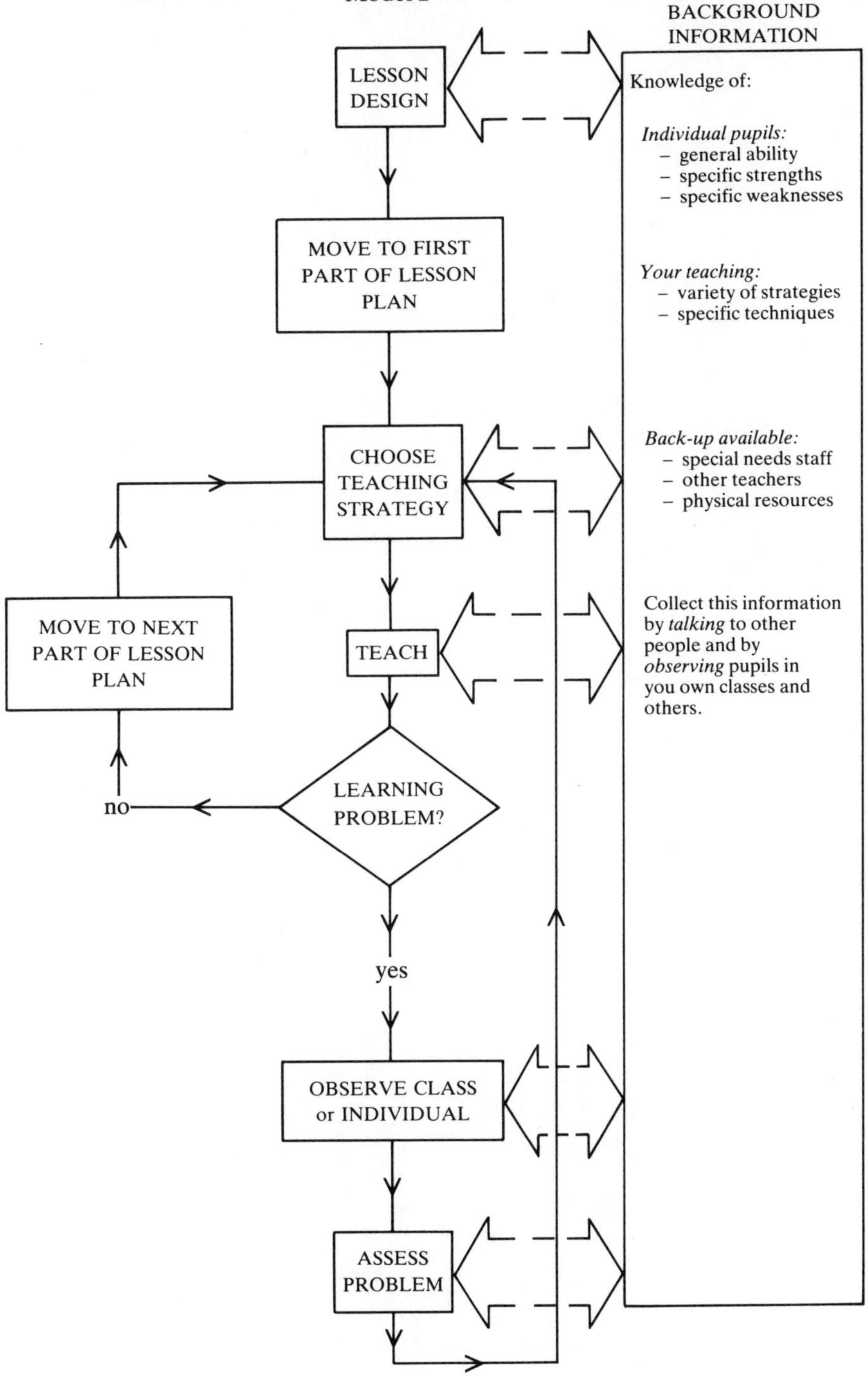

BACKGROUND
INFORMATION

```
┌──────────┐
│ LESSON   │ ⇔ ┅┅⇨
│ DESIGN   │ ⇔ ┅┅⇨
└────┬─────┘
     │
     ▼
┌──────────────┐
│ MOVE TO FIRST│
│ PART OF LESSON│
│    PLAN      │
└──────────────┘
```

Knowledge of:

Individual pupils:
  – general ability
  – specific strengths
  – specific weaknesses

Your teaching:
  – variety of strategies
  – specific techniques

```
┌──────────┐
│ CHOOSE   │ ⇔ ┅┅⇨
│ TEACHING │ ⇐───
│ STRATEGY │ ⇔ ┅┅⇨
└────┬─────┘
     │
     ▼
┌──────────┐
│  TEACH   │ ⇔ ┅┅⇨
└────┬─────┘
     │
     ▼
   ◇ LEARNING
     PROBLEM?  ──no──→
     │
    yes
     │
     ▼
┌──────────────┐
│ OBSERVE CLASS│ ⇔ ┅┅⇨
│ or INDIVIDUAL│ ⇔ ┅┅⇨
└──────────────┘
     │
     ▼
┌──────────┐
│ ASSESS   │ ⇔ ┅┅⇨
│ PROBLEM  │ ⇔ ┅┅⇨
└──────────┘
```

Back-up available:
  – special needs staff
  – other teachers
  – physical resources

Collect this information
by *talking* to other
people and by
observing pupils in
you own classes and
others.

```
┌──────────────┐
│ MOVE TO NEXT │
│ PART OF LESSON│
│    PLAN      │
└──────────────┘
```

Bibliography

APU, 1980, 1981, 1982a, *Mathematical Development Secondary Survey Reports 1, 2 & 3,* London, HMSO.

APU, 1982b, *Science in Schools, Age 13: Report No 1,* London, HMSO.

Arbitman-Smith, R., Haywood, H.C. & Bransford, J.D., 1984, 'Assessing cognitive change', in Brooks, P.H. *et al* (eds), *Learning and cognition in the mentally retarded,* Hillsdale, LEA.

Arnold, H., 1982, *Listening to children read,* London, Hodder & Stoughton.

Ashman, A.F., 1984, 'The cognitive abilities of the moderately and severely retarded', in Kirby, J.R., *Cognitive strategies and educational performance,* London, Academic Press.

Bell, P. & Kerry, T., 1982, *Teaching Slow Learners in Mixed Ability Classes,* Basingstoke, Macmillan.

Bentley, C. & Malvern, D., 1983, *Guides to assessment in education: mathematics,* London, Macmillan.

Blackman, L.S. & Lin, A., 1984, 'Generalisation training in the educable mentally retarded: intelligence and its educability revisited', in Brooks, P.H. *et al* (eds), *Learning and cognition in the mentally retarded,* Hillsdale, LEA.

Campione, J.C., Brown, A.L. & Ferrara, R.A., 1982, 'Mental retardation and intelligence', in Sternberg, R.J. (ed), *Handbook of human intelligence,* Cambridge, Cambridge University Press.

Cronbach, L.J. & Snow, R.E., 1977, *Aptitudes and Instructional Methods,* New York, Irvington.

Cripps C., 1983, *The teaching of spelling,* London, National Association for Remedial Education.

Davies, F. & Greene, T., 1984, *Reading for learning in the sciences,* London, Schools Council, Oliver and Boyd.

DES, 1975, *A Language for Life* (Bullock Report), London HMSO.

DES, 1978, *Report of the Committee of Enquiry into the Education of Handicapped Children and Young People* (Warnock Report), London, Department of Education and Science.

DES, 1982, *Report of the Committee of Inquiry into the Teaching of Mathematics in Schools,* (Cockroft Report), London, HMSO.

Feuerstein, R. *et al,* 1980, *Instrumental Enrichment, an intervention program for cognitive modifiability,* Baltimore, University Park Press.

Fish, J., 1985, *Special Education: The Way Ahead,* Milton Keynes, Open University Press.

72

Gordon, N. & McKinlay, I., 1980, *Helping clumsy children,* London, Churchill Livingstone.

Graham, K.G. & Robinson, H.A., 1984, *Study skills handbook,* International Reading Association.

Gulliland, J., 1972, *Readability,* London, Hodder and Stoughton.

Harrison, C., 1980, *Readability in the classroom,* Cambridge, Cambridge University Press.

Kerslake, D., 1982, 'Talking about mathematics', in Harvey, R. *et al, Language Teaching and Learning: Mathematics,* (Book 6 in the series Language Teaching and Learning edited by Torbe, M.) London, Ward Lock Educational.

Leah, M., 1982, 'Using Computer Assisted Learning to Implement Spelling across the Curriculum', Unpublished M.A., University of Reading.

Longley, C., 1977, *Reading after ten,* London, BBC.

Lunzer, E. & Gardner, K., 1979, *The effective use of reading,* London, Schools Council, Heinemann.

Lunzer, E. & Gardner, K., 1984, *Learning from the written word,* London, Schools Council, Oliver and Boyd.

Morris, A. & Stewart-Dore, N., 1984, *Learning to learn from text,* London, Addison-Wesley.

Nussbaum, J. & Norvick, S., 1981, 'Brainstorming in the classroom to invent a model: a case study', *School Science Review, 62, 221,* 771–8.

Perera, K., 1980, 'The assessment of linguistic difficulty in reading material', *Educational Review, 32,2,* 151–61.

Perera, K., 1986, 'Some linguistic difficulties in school subjects', in Gillham, B. (ed), *The language of school subjects,* London, Heinemann,

Peters, M., 1985, *Spelling caught or taught: a new look,* London, Routledge and Kegan Paul.

Rees, R. & Barr, G., 1984, *Diagnosis and prescription. Some common maths problems,* London, Harper and Row.

Sassoon, R., 1983, *The practical guide to children's handwriting,* London, Thames and Hudson.

Simpson, M. & Arnold, B., 1982, 'Educational psychology and the teaching of specialist subjects, *Scottish Educational Review 14,2,* 109–17.

Spencer, E., 1983, *Writing matters: across the curriculum,* London, Hodder and Stoughton/SCRE.

Sternberg, R.J., 1984, 'Macrocomponents and microcomponents of intelligence: some proposed loci of mental retardation', in Brooks, P.H. *et al* (eds), *Learning and cognition in the mentally retarded,* Hillsdale, LEA.

Swann, W., 1983, 'Curriculum Principles for Integration', in Booth, T, & Potts, P., *Integrated Special Education,* Oxford, Basil Blackwell.

Thornton, G., 1980, *Teaching writing,* London, Edward Arnold.

Weber, K.J., 1978, *Yes, they can!,* Milton Keynes, Open University Press.

Williams, A.A., 1985, 'Success in mathematics', in Smith, C.J.(ed), *New directions in remedial teaching,* Lewes, The Falmer Press.

Notes for tutors

Introduction

These notes have been written to give tutors and group leaders a few ideas about how to use the material in this book with their students. Initially the book was written for pre-service students, but it can equally well be adapted for use during formal or informal in-service activities. We are thinking particularly of activities for probationary teachers who are dealing with special needs pupils in their classrooms for the first time, and activities for other staff who have chosen to make this the focus of their professional development for a while. This book will be helpful to any of these groups who need practical help in meeting some of their pupils' *learning* needs. Other books in this series deal with other parts of the special needs field.

Specific ideas for tutors

1) Sensitising students

Activity 1.1 on page 4 of the main text provides students (a term which we shall use to refer to those involved in both pre-service and in-service study) with some useful experiences on which to base their work on learning difficulties. If possible, tutors should ask those who will be taking part in sessions on this topic to carry out this activity *before* the series of sessions begins and should refer to what students have found out as the series unfolds.

2) Looking at special needs pupils

Ask each member of the group to report on a special needs pupil from their own experience in mainstream classes. Collect this information on the board, or on an OHP, under the following headings: pupil's sex; nature of the learning difficulty; one other non-academic characteristic. This list will provide the basis for further discussion concerning some of the more frequently found difficulties and act as a reason for looking into the text to find ways of responding to the difficulties mentioned. It may also indicate the need for more detailed diagnosis of learning problems which can stimulate reference to the checklists and associated activities in Chapter 2.

Also, the listed non-academic characteristics of children with learning problems can be revealing. There will often be an imbalance in terms of the number of boys and girls who have been mentioned. This can prompt interesting consideration of what teachers are responding to in identifying that a child has a learning problem. There may also be several comments on disruptive behaviour which can be followed up by reference to the book on that topic in this series.

3) Looking at a lesson

Ask the students to bring along notes of a lesson which they plan to teach. Then invite them to list the demands of this lesson under three headings: language and literacy; numeracy; concepts required (at what level?). This may be quite difficult to do at first and may work best by getting the group to work as pairs, the two students in the pair being teachers of the same subject. After analysing a lesson in this way, decisions need to be taken concerning what kinds of support diffferent pupils in the class will need during that lesson. Chapters 3–7 give a range of ideas for support. Consideration will also need to be given to the kinds of classroom organisation which will best enable the teacher to deploy these support strategies. The group might consider, for example, the particular constraints and opportunities offered by group, individual or whole class work. It may be particularly helpful, during this consideration of a lesson, to focus in the first instance on the individual pupils who were discussed in (2) above.

In a later session, students should report on what happened when they taught the lesson, reflecting on such things as the practicability and acceptability of the strategies they tried, on how (if at all) they had to adapt the strategy and why, and on the extent to which other things which they did in the lesson might be judged in relation to the ideas presented elsewhere in this book. In this way both the ideas and the day to day practice of the student are subjected to constructive criticism through which progress towards better special needs practice might be made.

4) Looking at classroom resources

During this session, students are invited to bring along resource materials for a lesson which they have planned. This could be a text book, worksheet, set of instructions or whatever. Working in pairs, the two students in each pair being from different subject disciplines, they should be asked to focus on the demands of these materials, and what, in particular, pupils may find difficult either in understanding or acting on the information. Chapters 3–7 (and especially Chapter 6) will help to inform this activity.

Mixed subject pairs have several advantages for this work:

a) both members of the pair will not be equally familiar with the content, so things on a physics worksheet which might be taken for granted by two physicists might be recognised as ambiguous or difficult by a historian working with a physicist;

b) the pair will bring different skills to the task — so a physicist might be able to help the historian to recognise the numeracy difficulties inherent in a history worksheet.

After the materials discussed in this session have been used with pupils, there might again be a debriefing session of the kind discussed under (3) above.

5) Looking at classroom management

Tutors should try to make arrangements whereby students could visit other teachers' classes to see how they include pupils with special needs (especially those with learning difficulties) in their lessons. What techniques do they use to settle the class down to work? How do they organise themselves for giving individual support to certain pupils? How do they modify their resources to maximise the learning opportunities of those pupils? How do they group pupils for collaborative activities? Are all pupils with difficulties kept together (and perhaps given different work)?

If possible there should be an opportunity for the students to talk with the teachers afterwards. It would be of interest for them to ask what the teachers would like to do to make provision for pupils with learning difficulties within their lessons, what is practicable and acceptable, what constraints operate, what opportunities can be exploited (e.g. through the use of in-class helpers).

In a debriefing session students should be encouraged to discuss what they have seen and heard of other teachers' practice and to reflect on how they might personally try to bring the sort of support strategies that they have studied in earlier sessions into play in their own lessons. The enquiry-based model of teaching presented in the last chapter of this book might also be discussed at this stage.

6) Seeking help

It is not expected that every teacher will know everything there is to know about helping pupils with learning difficulties — especially pupils with the more severe problems. However, there are specialist staff in every school who are able to help individual pupils and the mainstream teacher. In order that students can make best use of advice from such staff, their attention should be drawn to the procedures suggested in Chapter 8.

Having tried this out in their own schools (or teaching practice schools) students should report back on the value of their consultations with specialist staff.

7) Things to think about

Tutors might like to ask students to consider the following points to help to set their thinking on pupils with learning difficulties into a broader special needs context.

a) What organisational strategies could ordinary schools adopt to help them to deal successfully with children with special educational needs?
Consider the following suggestions (and ask — are there others?)

Special needs children

1. Could be educated in a totally separate unit on the site of the main school.

2. Could be in tutor groups in the main school but have all their lessons in a separate unit taught by unit staff.

3. Could be in separate classes in the main school taught by the main school staff.

4. Could be based in ordinary classes but be withdrawn for special help when necessary, either in small groups or individually.

5. Could be supported in ordinary classes by the presence of an extra teacher (or helper) whose main duty was to help those children.

What do the students think about the various approaches? Is there one 'right' approach?

b) What are the pros and cons of integrating children with severe difficulties into ordinary schools?

c) What changes in the basic ways in which schools function, would make it easier to meet the needs of children with learning difficulties?

d) What kinds of children are likely to have special educational needs?

It may help to ask what kinds of children will have special needs during oral work, during written work, in Science or Craft, during tutor group sessions, in P.E., in connection with extra curricular activities or when it comes to choosing options in the Upper School?

Students will find helpful information in *Organising the School's Response* in this series.

8) Subject specific resources

The following publications are a selection of those which are available for reference. They are listed under subject headings:

English

Mills, R.W., 1977, *Teaching English Across the Ability Range,* Ward Lock.
Walsh, B., 1983, 'The Basics and "Remedial" English' in R. Harrison (ed), *English Studies 11–18,* Hodder & Stoughton.

Mathematics

Biddle, A., Savage, S., Smith, T. & Vowles, 1985, L., *Mathematics for Low Attainers,* West Sussex County Council.
Briggs, E., 1984, *Teaching Mathematics 7–13, Slow Learning and Able Children,* NFER-Nelson.
Harvey, R., Kerslake, D., Shuard, H. & Torre, M., 1982, *Mathematics,* Language Learning and Teaching Series No. 6, M. Torbe (ed), Ward Lock.
Struggle — Mathematics for low attainers, Distributed by ILEA, c/o Harry Hewitt, Teacher's Centre for Special Education, Webber Row, London, SE1 8QW, 01–261–1824

Geography

Boardman, D., 1982, *Geography with Slow Learners,* Geographical Association: Sheffield.
Corney, G. & Rawling, E., 1985, *Teaching Slow Learners through Geography,* Geographical Association: Sheffield.

History

Cowie, E.B., "History and the Slow-learning child", The Historical Association.
McIver, V., (ed), 1982, *Teaching History to Slow Learning Children in Secondary Schools,* Learning Resources Unit, Stranmillis College, Belfast.

McMinn, R., 1983, *Teaching History to Slow Learning Children in Secondary Schools,* Stranmillis College, Belfast.
Nichol, J., 1984, *Teaching History,* Macmillan.

Music

Dobes, J.P.B., 1966, *The Slow Learner and Music,* Oxford University Press.
Dobes, J.P.B., 1967, 'Music in Special Education', *Music,* Vol. No. 3, pp. 17–20.
Ward, D., 1976, *Hearts, Hands and Voices: Music in the education of slow learners,* Oxford University Press.

Science

Bulman, L., 1985, *Teaching language and study skills in secondary science,* Heinemann.
Cassells, J. & Johnson, A., 1980, *Understanding of Non-Technical Words in Science,* The Chemical Society.
Davies, F. & Greene, T., 1984, *Reading for Learning in the Sciences,* Oliver & Boyd/Schools Council.
Jones A.V., 1983, *Science for Handicapped Children,* Souvenir Press.
Kincaid, D., Rapson, H. & Richards, R., 1983, *Science for Children with Learning Difficulties,* Schools Council/Macdonald Education.
Schools Council., 1983, *Science for children with Learning Difficulties:* A Unit for Teachers 'Learning Through Science', Macdonald Education/Schools Council.

Modern Languages

Carson, D., 1980, 'Provision for the Less Able in S3 and S4', *Modern Langauges in Scotland,* No. 20, pp. 59–64.
CILT, 1972, *Teaching Modern Languages across the Ability Range.*
Scottish Education Department, 1970, *Modern Languages for the less Able Pupil.*
Smith, D.G., 1973, 'French and the Less Able', *Modern Languages,* Vol. 4, No. 4, pp. 105–115.

Computers

Behrmann, M., 1984, *Handbook of Microcomputers in Special Education,* NFER Nelson/College Hill Press.
M.E.P., *Micro Primer Pack for Special Needs,* MEP Small projects in South West, e.g. 'Word Processing in Special Schools',
Rostron, A. & Sewell, D., 1983, *Microtechnology in Special Education,* Croom Helm.

Index